DEAR SURVIVORS

DEAR SURVIVORS
Planning after Nuclear Holocaust: War Avoidance

John Burton

Frances Pinter (Publishers), London
Westview Press, Boulder, Colorado

© John Burton, 1982

First published in Great Britain in 1982 by
Frances Printer (Publishers) Ltd
5 Dryden Street, London WC2E 9NW

ISBN 0 86187 265 7 hardback
     0 86187 266 5 paperback

Published in the United States of America by
Westview Press, Inc.
5500 Central Avenue
Boulder, Colorado 80301
Frederick A. Praeger, President and Publisher

Library of Congress Cataloging in Publication Data

Burton, John, 1915-
   Dear survivors.

   Bibliography: p.
   1. War. 2. Civilization, Modern--1950-
3. World politics--1975-1985. 4. Atomic warfare.
5. World War III. I. Title.
U21.2.B87   1982   335'.028   82-50666
ISBN 0-86531-455-1
ISBN 0-86531-456-X (pbk.)

Typeset by Joshua Associates, Oxford
Printed by SRP, Exeter, Great Britain

This letter is addressed to you, officials, in your shelters . . .

John Burton

CONTENTS

Preface	ix
THE LETTER	1
PART I: DEFINING THE PROBLEM	8
Why We Failed in 1945	8
An Objective Basis	20
The Consensus of Assumptions	43
Needs Theory Applied to Industry	56
Needs Theory Applied to Political Relations	75
How to Reason	84
PART II: WAR AVOIDANCE POLICIES	100
System Imperatives	100
The Second Track	105
The Role of Middle Powers	112
Problem Solving	115
The 'Is' and the 'Ought'	125
Some Propositions and Conclusions	127
Bibliography	135

PREFACE

No doubt it concentrates the mind to be in a bomb shelter awaiting the 'All Clear' after a thermonuclear war. There is little time to consider post-war planning—unlike last time when there were four or five years. Cleaning up and reconstruction will be the immediate concern; but, as happened after World War II, this merely leads to business as usual and to the continuation of the problems that finally lead to disaster. Something more forward-looking than reconstruction is required—planning war avoidance in the future and the conditions of peaceful relationships. This epistle invites you to think ahead. Maybe if we had simulated life in a bomb shelter and had thought about the future in such a condition there could have been war avoidance without the experience of the holocaust of World War III.

John Burton

THE LETTER

Dear Survivors

First let me give you an outline of what I plan to do in this letter. After World War II many of us were actively engaged in 'post-war reconstruction'. Indeed, the exercise commenced well before 1945: we had two or three years of planning because that war, unlike this, lasted for five years. The holocaust of World War III was a direct result of our failures: despite the opportunity to plan in advance (an opportunity you do not have) we went about making the necessary immediate adjustments to get the economic system back to 'normal' and the inter-State and colonial systems reinstated along pre-war lines, without realizing that by going back to 'business as usual' we were inevitably inviting conflict in the future. We, in effect, set about re-creating the conditions that had led to that war—and to World War I. We failed, as I shall argue in my first section, because there was no knowledge base on which to work. We did not fully understand what started war in the first place, except in the most superficial terms about Germans, Italians, Japanese and their leaderships. On the other hand, by the 1980s there was no intellectual excuse for failure to avoid war in the future. You, in your predicament, for which you as leaders and administrators on both sides of the conflict are responsible, will not agree with this conclusion, but I hope I can convince you.

However, your main problem now while you wait for the 'All Clear', is for you to determine your objectives. What are your goals? How are you to avoid the pre-World War III problems associated with ideologies as the basis of political decisions? Is there no objective means of arriving at goals that are attainable and policies that succeed? This is the subject of my next section. I call it 'An Objective Basis'. In it I suggest that in the 1970s we had come to the conclusion—too late to prevent what has now happened—that there are certain basic and universal human needs that have to be satisfied if the individual and group are to be harmonious members of their wider societies. These needs offer objective goals and bases for policy-making.

Just to underline this argument I go on to discuss several consensual assumptions that were the bases of policies, but were clearly false. This is to convince you that it is important for authorities to encourage fundamental thinking about social and political relationships and to take note of its outcomes—stifle thought or ignore thought and policies go haywire. The socialist countries tended to do this; but they were not alone. It was tragic in the West, when governments began widespread cutbacks to education and research in social and political areas, and to favour instead technological training in the 1970s. This was the market 'wants' ideology prevailing over 'needs'—just when we were beginning to make progress and to explore some important new ideas.

To make what is argued more realistic I have devoted the next two parts of this epistle to applications in industrial relations and in political relations. This is merely to demonstrate that intellectual thinking is not necessarily ivory-tower stuff, as many of you claimed when I tried to have discussions with you in the decade before World War III.

I think it is worth considering why our thinking was so primitive for so long. Civilizations are only babies, it is true; but there seems to be, in retrospect, very little justification for the slow advances in political thought as compared with the tremendous strides taken in technological thinking. However, one reason was resources: far more man-hours were devoted to technology than to problems of human relationships—largely because of the general interest in market wants rather than in human needs. Another more fundamental reason seems to have been a methodological one. How should we have tried to acquire the necessary knowledge? We did not spend enough time on learning how to think, especially in respect of the more complex problems of human relationships. Simple ideas and examples are adequate for most physical science problems and technological development, but we did not get down to thinking about human relationships as a scientific or logical challenge. We were prepared to content ourselves with an ideological approach. There were some far-out philosophers, notably Kuhn and Popper, who thought more widely, but got it wrong because they had little actual experience or contact with those who did have real experience and who were facing practical problems in research or in application. In the next section I discuss these issues. Don't pass it over, even though it seems a bit beside the point when you are thinking about cleaning up the mess, because if you get this wrong you get the lot wrong. If only we had taught how to reason right through from primary to university education, things would have been different. In practice this approach was rarely taught even at universities. Worse still, university teaching itself was usually conducted in total ignorance of some of these important philosophical considerations, which resulted in teachers and students arriving at false conclusions in many fields important to the study of human relationships.

This brings me to the end of Part I of this epistle, which I call 'Defining the Problem'. Part II is concerned with 'War Avoidance Policies'.

You will, when you emerge, be so concerned with the immediate problems of law and order, survival and administration that you will be led step-by-step back into forms of organization that prevent you carrying out whatever long-term plans you may have thought about while in your shelters: the way you handle the first few days will determine to a large degree the forms of social and political organization that will evolve. There are 'system processes' that take decision-making out of your control. Take, for example, the decision that was one link in the chain of events that led to this nuclear holocaust: the attack on the President of the United States in 1981. It became obvious at that time that communication links could be disrupted by such an event, and the decision was made to give a final power of decision to the officers in control of retaliation. This was a logical, rational, administrative arrangement to make. There was no other logical decision possible. You will find, when you are cleaning up, that one decision leads to another. Unless you have a plan that is thought out in advance, unless your decisions are based on some objective principles and goals that you have discovered and thought through in advance, unless you are committed to your goals and their pursuit to the extent that you will not allow institutional demands to frustrate human needs, without knowing it you will be a slave to decision processes. My next section, called 'System Imperatives', deals with some of these issues.

This letter is addressed, of course, to all of you emerging from shelters, wherever you are. If you all think your positions through, knowing that others are doing the same, relationships could be on a common and harmonious base. That is why I am getting this epistle into shelters on both sides of the divide. But remember that when you emerge you will be emerging in a cultural context—conflagration will not have changed this. There will not be agreement on why World War III started. You will be inclined to blame each other. Be careful of this. You can easily get back into that terrible frame of mind of the pre-World War III period. You all thought that you were involved in a win–lose confrontation (in which all would be losers in real terms). It did not

THE LETTER

seem to occur to anyone in authority that, far from this being the case, your relationships were potentially positive-sum—the more security each had the more the other could experience, the more one helped the other solve its internal and external problems the less likely would there be any conflict from which all would suffer. You remember how you in the West argued that you had to support repressive and violent authorities when they were on your side in case the Eastern bloc intervened and took over? In the light of what happened this was clearly self-defeating. Remember how both sides tried to take advantage of the internal problems of the other? This was also self-defeating. However, if you do get misled into policies that turn out to be conflictual, as is almost inevitable, do not be diverted wholly into defensive stances. There are positive steps that can be taken alongside defence. My next section is a plea to you decision makers along these lines. It is called 'The Second Track'—not an alternative to defence, but a complementary approach.

Some groups are bound to have more resources than others, and these stronger groups or nations will try to dominate each other. Part of the Second Track involves a special role for 'Middle Powers'. My next section is devoted to this role. Before this war there was a great debate, especially in Western Europe, on the role of middle Powers such as Britain. American leaders referred to it as 'dangerous pacifism'. However, it was an ill-informed debate, confusing neutrality, independence, unilateral actions, disarmament, no foreign bases and other related issues. The role of middle Powers should be thought out in the context of the type of inter-State system that is bound to emerge once again.

You will run into problems no matter how careful you are. Mistakes will be made, unanticipated accidents will occur and conflicts result. They are inevitable. What you must have, therefore, are adequate processes for dealing with disputes well before they have any chance of becoming violent or destructive ones. I call this 'problem solving', which I spell out in some detail.

Ideas such as a 'Second Track' are sometimes regarded as 'controversial' even among scholars—many of whom have vested interests in old habits of thought and even ideological interests. No idea deserves the label 'controversial', at least without consideration and, perhaps, not even then. Ideas are usually part true and part false. They can be subjected to analysis; but it is most difficult to establish finally what is true and what is false. Initially, the benefit of doubt should be given to the creator of ideas. However, in trying to make a judgement it is important to separate the 'is' from the 'ought'. So often the 'controversial' is discarded because it is regarded as unrealistic. But so often 'realists' are, on reflection, talking in the unrealistic world of 'oughts', so pervasive is ideological and cultural thinking. Intellectuals are part of the elite group in any society. Decision makers are another part of the same elite group. The 'oughts' of society are the 'oughts' of elites and of people who would like to think that what they stand for is the 'is'. My next section contains this warning because you survivors are drawn from elite groups: you are likely to operate on the basis of a 'consensus'. This could lead you into a lot of trouble even in dealing with your own domestic relationships, because what you believe to be a consensus may be a set of false assumptions.

I do not want to make judgements about what happened. There was a series of events and accidents and no one will ever be able to get all the facts clear, let alone interpret them reliably. You have to adopt a 'no fault' approach. On the other hand, on both sides there were some obvious faults inherent in the various political and economic systems—you must have been aware of them, even though not acknowledging them as faults. These were institutional faults, if you like, rather than personal faults. In the next part I want to bring together some of what has been argued earlier by pointing to these institutional faults. They have to be avoided at all costs in the world you manage to build. In particular, one side was directed by market demands for wants and the other was directed by what was thought—sometimes mistakenly—were needs. Both got it wrong for different reasons which we will explore.

You will find, Dear Survivors, that I stress the human needs idea repeatedly in these pages. This is because the idea developed only in the decade before World War III and ideas take time to mature. It is useful to re-state it in different contexts. The need idea is the basic idea in this epistle—all else follows from it. It emerged clearly in the 1970s to give an objective basis for thought and policy, and it is therefore well worth repeating.

Have a look back at the table of contents of this letter. You will see in title form the general plan and perhaps you will not get so bored with what at first sight appears to be remote from your immediate administrative and occupational concerns. You do not have much time: thinking out a future like this, thinking about war avoidance, in the face of tradition, convention, culture and ideology is a long process. We found before this war that students took several years to break habits of thought and to question and to re-think. You are adults and your thought patterns are even more deeply ingrained. Even after students did succeed in questioning, new ideas and new orientations had to sit like wine in bottles to mature. You do not have this time. The only way to substitute for the maturing process of time is to discuss, debate, argue, mull, contemplate. As we were warned just before World War II: 'Think or be damned!'

THE LETTER

PART I DEFINING THE PROBLEM

Why We Failed in 1945

My purpose in this opening passage is to look back, to assess success and failure over forty years and to see whether there are some lessons to be learnt that might be useful to present and future administrations and governments.

Prior to World War III there was a cynicism on the part of many people and general absence of direction and commitment on the part of senior administrators and political leaders. Whereas many of the post-World War II generation of administrators were caught up in a challenging post-war situation and were able to be creative to some degree in that politically permissive and euphoric reconstruction period, pre-catastrophe advisers, such as you, seemed to be more resigned to fate and to failure. Was the post-World War II period really one of opportunity and if so why did we fail? Forty years later was there a degree of political and social realism that we lacked in the 1940s? Are there, in practice, no answers to public policy problems other than reactive and opportunistic ones? Unemployment, inflation, deprivation and poverty, discrimination, communal conflicts, high incidence of 'deviance', growing inequalities of incomes and opportunities within and between nation-States—are all of these conditions inevitable in human societies? They give rise to major conflicts and wars; must we accept these as part of some historical process? Or does public administration include possible choices and reliable means by which these can be determined and achieved? Is there a 'science' of policy making? Was the state of resignation in the pre-holocaust period due to an objective impossibility of solving problems by deliberate intervention, or was it due to a lack of knowledge, an unawareness of the existing knowledge about human behaviour and problem solving processes?

THE LETTER

My argument for you to consider before you emerge is that:

(i) in the post-World War II period there was no basic knowledge available which could be used to solve the problems confronting the post-World War II world;
(ii) this was not just because of personal ignorance, but because there was no such knowledge existing in the thought of the period;
(iii) after 1950 there was a shift in thinking of a fundamental nature;
(iv) this provided both a theoretical framework and the processes relevant to the handling of problems that emerged during this forty-year period;
(v) this shift created a knowledge gap between the actual and the potential core of knowledge available to practitioners; and
(vi) this knowledge gap could have been bridged by a fundamental restructuring of preparatory and in-service training of administrators and closer links between scholars and administrators.

The absence of a knowledge base

To us in the post-World War II period there were relatively simple answers to relatively simple questions. In the international field we were pleased with the outcome of the 1945 Charter Conference and the many amendments to the Dumbarton Oaks draft that it was possible to introduce. In retrospect, in the light of developments and present knowledge, this was a misconceived document based on a misconceived perception of world society. The United Nations was little more than a means of legitimizing and protecting a great number of non-legitimized authorities, few of whom had effective authority within their own boundaries and all of whom (even acting together) could not solve problems of conflict. On the domestic front we assumed that if governments were so inclined they could bring about conditions of full employment by simple budgetary policies, and that these policies would not fundamentally alter the income distribution or the structure of the economy. We have failed to perceive, because we lacked an adequate theoretical framework, several important trends:

First, we were confronted with a growing devolution within nation-States, with a consequent loss of authority by central governments. Whereas we were once confident that governments, on the basis of their constitutions, could plan effectively, in practice central authorities did not have the capabilities we assumed they had. Control of monetary supply in Britain was no easier than was the control of strikes in Poland. The erosion of authority was common to all political systems and all social levels. Why this was so and whether it was to be welcomed or not, need not concern us here. The 1980s administrators and governments were dealing with an ambiguous authority situation and had a more limited idea of policy possibilities.

Second, while we anticipated increased and effective planning, by 1970—if not earlier—there emerged a stage at which both *laissez faire* and planned systems had failed in their own ways. Unemployment, inflation, and inequalities, on the one hand, and a lack of participation coupled with a remote bureaucratic elite, on the other, were two of the symptoms of failure. Even so, no third system emerged, no alternative to *laissez faire* or planning. There were no models for the future. The 1980s ideologies, conservative and radical, were still the ideologies of a past century. In the absence of a model or a new ideology there were no guide lines for governments. Although the ideas of smallness, participation, equality, the absence of 'we–they' relations in industry and of consensus government existed, there was no idealized society that brought all these together.

Third, the international system became more interdependent than we imagined it would be. Private organizations could determine the behaviour of some nation-States. Independent foreign policies, economic, political and strategic, were not possible, even for major nation-States. We, on the other hand, had thought that we lived in a world that comprised independent nation-States, each with effective authority and decision making latitude within its own boundaries.

Having failed to anticipate these major developments, by the 1950s we were experiencing major problems at all levels: a growing threat of major East–West international conflict, many minor wars between neighbouring nations, over 130 minority–majority disputes within nation-States, internal instability in the majority of developing nations, high levels of violence within developed nations, growing inequalities of income and the dismantling of the welfare state where it had taken shape, major diversions of resources to defence, failure to employ unemployed resources in education, health and other services, and so on. All this must be regarded as failure consequent upon planning or the absence of it in the post-World War II reconstruction period.

In retrospect, the inadequate framework in which we operated and which prevented us anticipating these developments and problems is clear: it was the classical one that had gone unchallenged for centuries. We assumed that every nation-State was independent, that international problems could be separated from national, that there was a reserved area of domestic jurisdiction. By contrast, the world that emerged in the second half of the century included nation-States with minorities that had close ties with nationals of other States, there were international concerns about human rights, there were industrial and strategic networks that cut across State boundaries, and there were the international consequences of non-legitimized authorities which survived thanks only to external support. At the domestic level, the classical assumption was that there are those who have the right to expect obedience and those who have an obligation to obey. This gave rise to many curious applications of law and order, including the legality accorded to authorities in effective control despite the means exercised, and the distortion of the notion of democracy to justify majority rule even when there were ethnic minorities. Associated with this notion of authority, classical thought included the assumption that societies were integrated wholes. There were two schools of thought, 'coercion' theorists and value theorists. Both endeavoured to explain integration without consideration of the assumption of integration itself. Why assume societies are integrated wholes or that their members wish to be integrated? A logical extension of this thinking was that threat and punishment must be used to enforce social norms whenever the individual was not socialized by other means into accepting them.

Little wonder, then, that post-World War II reconstruction included an acceptance of coercion politics as the basis of the all-pervasive theoretical framework; judicial settlement, power bargaining and negotiation as the appropriate decision making process; and adversary parliamentary, industrial and law and order systems as the institutional foundations. It was within this classical conception of social organization that we operated, focusing on the immediate goals of a welfare state —which were unattainable in such a world.

At a more fundamental level, post-World War II reconstruction was conducted within a framework that took institutions as the unit of analysis and explanation of societies. It is a necessary assumption inherent in this view that each individual person is a malleable unit, subject to a socialization process. In this view it would be destructive to social stability and to 'law and order' if anyone had any inherent and objectively determined patterns of behaviour that could not be influenced and contained within the exising social structure.

It is not surprising, therefore, that the individual—as a participant in society—received little analytical attention. On the contrary, a special type of 'man' was invented to fit in with the theories and models of social and economic organization that had developed.

The view that this 'man' was or should be malleable was not confined to those seeking to maintain social systems. There were those who assumed the need for change toward egalitarianism, a redistribution of income and alterations in the control of production, who, even so, created a human being who had those interests, values and preferences that fitted their political ideologies. Whether the theorists looked towards conservation or revolution, in both cases the individual was assumed to be a malleable unit, one that was suited to the needs of the system. The goal could be either system preservation or system change; but in neither case was satisfaction of objectively determined human values or needs of primary importance.

The concern with organization and the absence of a concern for the requirements of individual human beings led to further attempts at 'integration'—more powers for authorities within nations and 'common markets' and regional federations in the international field. Integration was considered as having a positive value in itself, rather than in the human purposes it would either promote or prejudice.

A personal responsibility?

It will be clear that post-World War II reconstruction failure, resulting in the events that led up to World War III, was not the responsibility of administrators of that day. On the contrary, the challenges of World War II and of the post-1945 period attracted in many countries many of the outstanding theoreticians of the time and young people from universities. There was no great knowledge gap between theory and practice, between the available knowledge and applied knowledge. The existing knowledge base was itself inadequate to cope with the exponential acceleration of trends stimulated by the war. Independence movements, latent under colonialism, were released. A communications explosion made the experiences in one place a shared experience globally. The defence of structures within a traditional law and order framework, no matter how successful, were the cosmetics of the welfare state and could not be maintained. In retrospect, post-war reconstruction could not have succeeded on the existing knowledge base.

The shift in thinking

By the 1950s we were experiencing the consequences of World War II, in particular the domestic and international consequences of the rate of technological and political change. The two were connected. Communications promoted the spread of political change thus accelerating its rate. Independent movements and participatory demands in one place were therefore of world significance.

As is always the case, change in the outside world eventually stimulated analysis of this change. By the end of the 1950s there was a vast explosion of research within those disciplines trying to explain what was occurring. These early studies were primarily descriptive. They described and dealt with symptoms, they labelled, they reduced complex problems to puzzles by leaving out motivational variables. Policies were consistent with this approach. In the 1960s Northern Ireland was treated as a minority rebellion in a democratic State—it was as simple as that. The identity, ethnicity and participatory aspects were not thought to be relevant and, consequently, not taken into account in the policy that flowed from the definition. These studies were carried out within a traditional State centric model of society, which assumed that societies were integrated wholes or should be, that the general good was also the individual good, that there were those with a right to rule and those who had a moral obligation to obey. The focus of attention and the unit of analysis were institutions.

By the late 1960s, however, failure in almost every social and political field prompted reconsideration of many previously accepted assumptions. In the writings of the time the individual tended to be perceived as the independent variable and the unit of explanation. This was not the malleable and invented individual—economic man, legal man or ideological man—that so conveniently fitted whatever theory was being used. It was not the classical man whose interests were identical with those of the 'common good'. It was that individual who acted at all social levels, maximizing his individual satisfactions at all social levels, by any means that came to hand, legal or illegal. It was that individual who was involved in various types of conflict, from crime to war. It was that individual who was not deterred by threats and sanctions when acting separately or in a group or nation if his/her needs were at stake and who was constrained only by values attached to relationships. It was that individual who was being revealed more and more by experiences of crime, terrorism, co-operation and conformity at all social levels. It was that individual who had evolved over millions of years and had characteristics, motivations and needs that were universal over both time and space. It was that inconvenient individual who did not fit into any system just because others thought it was suited to his/her needs, because others tried to socialize or coerce, because others created structures that were in their view just. It was that individual who had an intelligence that required and *would* pursue, regardless of the consequences to anyone or anything, those conditions needed for survival and learning: consistency in response, recognition, identity, control or participation as a means of ensuring these needs were met. It was that individual who did not fit into serfdom, slavery, colonialism, capitalism or socialism. It was that real individual who was being discovered who found positive law and elite societies unacceptable—a very difficult and objectionable individual in any society that was not constucted by and for it.

A framework for political decisions

A shift in thinking of this significance could not take place without a clearly postulated theory. The theory that incorporated this interest in human behaviour into the earlier thinking on structures and power was one that hypothesized certain universal needs that were derived from learning theory, needs such as stimulus, security, identity, consistency of response and the need for control by the person of his/her environment as a means of pursuing these needs. It subsumed power theories because of the emphasis on control as a means toward need satisfaction. It explained the use of legal norms when they were suitable and the invention of others when they were not useful tools. The only constraints that existed were values attached to relationships. The conforming and the dissident, the normal and the abnormal, were comprehended within one theoretical framework. This 'control theory' and its applications at different social levels directed attention to conceptions and assumptions that were not usually subjected to re-examination. Later we will discuss some of these.

The practical or applied implications of this new approach to political theory were a significant shift in ideas on decision making (but not, alas, in practice), and a shift from the reactive, hierarchical type of decision making processes to interactive ones in which decisions emerge from the interaction of all affected parties. In this way, according to the theory, which we will spell out later, interests, values and needs are reflected in decisions.

However, it was in relation to participatory processes that the shift in thinking was most significant. In all relationships, whether 'good' or 'bad', it is only those involved who can judge which values are relevant, which patterns of behaviour are applicable. It is their interpretations of behaviour and events that create the reality. Clearly they are likely to alter their perceptions and interpretations with increased knowledge: if the processes of interaction include increased information by reason of increased communication between those concerned or injections of information by a third party, then the 'reality' may alter.

However, this was only theory: practitioners were not always aware of it. Let us take the example of economic and financial policy. Authorities had a choice—policies designed to deal with inflation by means that lead to unemployment and reduced services or policies designed to promote needs for education, health and the benefits of employment, stimulus, recognition, security and distributive justice. The former were designed to preserve the economic system. The latter would have required substantial income redistribution by progressive income tax and thus would have destroyed the system in some of its essential features. It was a choice made between, on the one hand, wants expressed in the articulate and influential market economy, and, on the other, the needs that are in evidence empirically and in theory, but which were not reflected in strong pressure groups. Western societies chose the former and the costs were reduced investments with all the consequences of disaffection, individual deviance and community violence. There was a spillover into the international community, especially when internal threat to the status quo provoked increased expenditure on police and the armed services and when unrest was thought to be foreign-inspired.

The same type of observation could be made in respect of policies relating to minorities and to industrial relations. There was the choice between preserving the we–they relations inherent in majority or management decision making, and inter-active decision making that alone could promote harmony of interests. In the post-World War II reconstruction period we were not sufficiently aware of the nature of we–they relations, of ethnicity, of identity and of participation. We planned on the basis of 'business as usual' in the post-World War II period. Come the World War III holocaust and the events leading to it, the evidence was clear how wrong we were. We had lacked an adequate theoretical base.

The knowledge gap

The 1980s administrators, on the other hand, were not justified in adopting a limited perspective on the role of authorities and in having such a high level of cynicism. Their problem was not an absolute lack of knowledge. Their problem was that there was an increasing knowledge gap between what was known and the actual knowledge of administrators and politicians. Looking back we could argue that despite our commitment much of our failure in the post-World War II reconstruction period was because of our massive ignorance. Our ignorance was in keeping with the scientific material of the time, coercion politics oriented, heavily weighted in favour of preserving structures and only a little concerned with problems of change. We relied on observation, pre-conceived ideologies and beliefs. We meant well and worked hard, but failed. However, the second half of the century saw a tremendous accumulation of knowledge —not just facts, but of theory—and a significant shift in thinking took place. Knowledge was available; but the knowledge gap appeared to get wider.

THE LETTER

It took at least five years for the fruits of new research to get into print in a readable form. It took another decade or so for such knowledge to be incorporated into teaching. There was then a gap of two or three decades, at the least, before teaching impinged on policy through the employment in influential positions of those taught. We were confronted with gaps of the order of 40 years.

On the basis of our experience, you looking to the future and to post-War World III planning, should be planning steps that seek to bridge this enormous gap between existing knowledge and applied knowledge. Libraries have a role. I suspect there was enough knowledge in libraries by which to solve most problems that confronted our societies. But try to synthesize it! I rather feel that we would have been better served if all books had been placed on shelves in the order in which they arrived or according to colour or size. Then we would have attached far more importance to means of extracting those bits of scattered knowledge that were relevant to the problems we were examining. The job of libraries should not have been just to accumulate books. More importantly it should have been to make the knowledge in those books available. A little of this was done by reference books and computers but not enough as it turns out.

A great deal more repeated in-service training was necessary, not just for those who wanted to escape for a short time from the routine of administration, but more particularly for those who did not want to. There was, also, a need for a far greater interchange between academics and administrators to their mutual advantage. Oh! that we had had a system whereby administrators reached their peak in salary and status by the age of 30 or 35 and, thereafter, were gradually demoted so that they retired at the status and salary at which they began!

An Objective Basis

This section is directed toward the problem of policy making. Can there be a 'scientific' (that is, objective) basis on which authoritative decisions can be made? The classical position—and, indeed, the position right up to World War III—was that there could not be a science of policy making because politics (being the authoritative distribution of resources) was concerned with value judgements. Competing ideologies, competing political parties, could base a programme on ethical considerations, cultural norms, consensus beliefs and values and on the 'general will'; but there could be no objective assessment of the differing goals, values and policies. The social and political scientist could present goal options, could point out what was not possible, could recommend alternative means to goals; but there was no basis on which priorities could be ordered other than the basis of value preferences.

This view I wholly reject. Political theorists came to an erroneous conclusion because they assumed the State or authorities to be the appropriate focus of attention and units of explanation. I would argue that if people within political organizations were taken as the units of analysis, then there would be certain facts or rules, which as in physics would always be true and would provide a basis for assessing policies; that there could, therefore, be a science of political theory and a philosophy of public policy (natural and social sciences have the same methods of approach); and that the tools of research and of policy making are processes whereby decision makers and people generally are in a position to observe the operation of these truths of behaviour.

The problem

The problem of public policy making was adequately stated by Brecht (1959). He described how at the beginning of the twentieth century the questions asked were 'What are the ends of State and government?' 'What are the means toward these ends?' 'What is the best form of government?' The answers, claimed at the time to be 'scientific', were in 'ought' terms: governments *ought* to serve the interests of the greatest number of individuals; States *ought* to be sovereign, and other such maxims. The twentieth-century scruples led scholars to believe that science implied facts, measurement and logical reasoning. Science as such could not, therefore, deal with political goals and means. Scholars could not even pass judgement on repression, cruelty or any behaviour of State authorities.

The problem can be stated in functional terms. Human societies were faced with high levels of violence, communal conflict, unemployment, inflation, industrial conflict, inequalities of income and opportunity, and wars. There were practical means of 'dealing with' these problems: repression and authoritative violence, arbitration, judicial settlements, power balances and deterrence. Trained 'scientists' were employed in advising on and implementing these policies, but only within given ideological value systems (you will recall how governments employed their own selection of advisers). Means of controlling inflation were recommended by economists despite the social and individual costs and consequences of unemployment. Minorities seeking recognition were suppressed by means recommended by trained strategists, within given ideologies. Social and political scientists had, in this classical and contemporary view, no objective basis on which to recommend solutions to these economic, social and political problems.

However, there is no logical deduced truth or law that states that there can be no objective assessment of public policy. The syllogism—public policy concerns subjective values, subjective values are not subject to scientific evaluation, therefore public policy is not subject to scientific evaluation—is based on what could be a false premise. Public policy could be concerned with subjective values, while also being concerned with over-riding behavioural traits that are constant and scientifically determined. That subjective values must be the basis of authoritative decision making is itself a subjective judgement that may be false.

The unit of explanation

The classical problem emerged once again in the latter half of the century because 'the State', authorities, the type of system and institutional structures had been the focus of attention and the units of analysis and explanation. As Brecht observed, the core political theory question posed was 'What is the best form of government?' Accordingly, political theory had been concerned primarily with organizations. In the classical view of society there were those who had a right to expect obedience and those who had a moral duty to obey (Lloyd, 1964). It was a necessary assumption inherent in this view that the individual was a malleable unit, subject to a socialization process.

It is not surprising, therefore, that the individual as a participant in society received little analytical attention. On the contrary, a special type of 'man' was invented to fit in with the theories and models of social organization that were developed. For example, economists invented 'economic man'—an individual or unit which could be a person, a firm or an industry. This unit was designed to have just those attributes that would be required by the smooth-running, self-regulating private enterprise system idealized by Western economists. The unit was suited to this system and the system was suited to it. The unit was rational, made choices and in so doing created this ideal type of economic system. The lawyer's individual, also, had the necessary attributes to benefit from and make ideal a system of law and order in which those in authority had a right to rule and others had a moral obligation to obey. 'Legal man' was rational and responded to the cost benefits of conformity and deterrents. Only the demented and the demonic were incapable of appreciating that it was in the common interest, and therefore the individual interest, to conform to the laws that prevailed. In the legal view society's interests and the interests of the individual were identical—even though society was managed by a class of people who had the right to govern and to coerce. Even the individual created by the psychologist prompted the question, why were only *some* individuals deviants? It seemed to be assumed that there were attributes of deviants that led them to confront the law. The 'normal' individual was conformist by nature and not by circumstances. Lack of development, of socialization, of moral character, of intelligence and of stability had, with some few exceptions, been held to be the main sources of social 'maladjustment' and non-conformity.

Two examples can be taken as illustrations of the two separate schools of thought, the one conserving and the other oriented toward change. In 1958 Winch believed that human behaviour at all social levels was governed by rules, these rules being the normal behaviour characteristic of various societies, cultures and relationships. He asserted, logically on the basis of his hypothesis, that 'the understanding of society is logically different from the understanding of nature'. Clearly, on his assumption that behaviour was governed by rules, he was right: there could not be any discernible patterns of behaviour and, therefore, there could be no science of behaviour. At best there could be generalizations about some of the behaviour of particular people at particular times in particular cultures and circumstances. This was an assumption that was inherent in classical legal thought: individuals conform to the law except in cases of diminished responsibility or immorality. The individual was not attributed with any inherent motives that inevitably led to deviant behaviour: society, its institutions and processes, deserved to be supported and preserved.

There was a more widespread school of thought that held that behaviour was rule-governed by reason of inexorable historical processes of change in the means of production and consequent changes in relationships between individuals in ruling and other classes. The historical processes provided the basis for generalizations and it was claimed, therefore, that the study of behaviour could be a scientific one. Whereas in the Winch case both the rules and the behaviour were subject to change over time and between cultures, in this case there were predictable environmental changes, at least over an historical period, that had predictable consequences for behaviour. Sue Himmelweil dealt with 'The individual as basic unit of analysis' in an interesting publication *Economics: An Anti-Text* published in 1977. She attacked orthodox economics, which rested so much on a unique economic man as the basic unit of analysis. But she did not endeavour to replace this invented man with a real one. On the contrary she threw away the individual, in every shape and form, in favour of 'economic systems as a whole'. She believed that there was a need for:

a theory of what determines people's tastes and how they do or do not change over time. . . . It is, therefore, the relations under which the surplus is produced and its use controlled that should be the basic tools of our analysis. . . . What we have is the individual within a class, under certain production relations, within a particular mode of production. To start with the individual is to start at the wrong end of the chain.

In her view the process of change in conditions from slavery to feudalism, to industrialization to socialism, is 'a process of class struggle, between the ruling (surplus-controlling) class of the old mode of production and the would-be ruling class of the new'.

Here we have, in the one case, an argument that behaviour was rule-governed, thus denying the possibility of any universality of behavioural patterns that could objectively be determined and, in the other case, the argument that changing production conditions promote altering class structures, which influence behaviour. In both cases the emphasis was on external conditions as the determining factors in behaviour and relationships. There appeared to be either an implicit or an explicit denial that there were any universal rules of behaviour that were universal by reason of any inherent individual behavioural propensities or patterns. In neither case did Winch or Himmelweil ask the question 'Why and how did the external conditions, which were thought to be the dominant variables, promote certain responses in the individual?' In both cases the assertion was that this malleable individual was capable of responses, unpredictable in the one case, predictable in the other, for reasons not explained outside some concept of malleability. An 'ideological man' joined his invented fellows.

My own personal observation might help to clarify the argument. In the 1930s, as a student of psychology and economics I believed that a more egalitarian economy was the means by which less divisive behaviour could be promoted within and between societies. The remedy was 'planning' at the initiative of central authorities. In this belief, behaviour related to 'structures'. The unit of analysis or explanation was structures. The ideal structure then being advocated, 'socialism', did not develop out of any consideration of human behaviour and individual values. As a consequence little, if any, thought was given to the participatory problems that emerged in the decade preceding World War III in large centralized political systems.

In summary, the rejection of orthodox models of the individual did not necessarily justify the rejection of the real individual as the unit of analysis. It could be that the individual, defined by reference to some universal human needs that would be pursued over the longer term, serves well as the basis of an explanation of social change. It could be that the pursuit of certain needs, such as identity and participation, undermined authoritative structures and was the source of political change in all technological conditions whenever or wherever these structures were compatible with such human needs.

The pre-World War III literature

Our experiences, including violent challenges to authorities, communal conflicts, industrial strikes and 'deviant' behaviour, forced us to challenge some classical assumptions. By the 1980s we could no longer assume that there was something natural and sanctified about 'legal' authority and its coercive institutions. We were forced by events to accept a notion of legitimacy based, not on legality, but upon the view that legitimacy is measured by the degree to which authorities and institutions serve those over whom authority is exercised and, in particular, to the degree to which they promote identity, development and a sense of fulfilment. Lack of legitimacy invites an explanation: there is a problem to be solved. This is not an observation based on idealism or humanitarianism. It is the political realistic observation that unless there is development and fulfilment of needs of individuals and groups, **unless** problems are solved and the need for coercion avoided, a social and political order may not be stable and harmonious, no matter what the level of coercion. Our experience of protest movements, violence throughout society, terrorism, civil conflicts, dissident behaviour, strikes, revolts, revolutions and wars were only visible symptoms and were a misleading clue to unseen motivations.

After about 1950, social and political science literature responded to these contemporary events with altering concepts, changing emphases and wider orientations, giving rise to alternative theories. These altering concepts reflected an inter-disciplinary—or is it an 'a-disciplinary'?—approach.

The whole individual—not separate economic, legal, psychological men—was being analysed. Concepts that were beginning to dominate thought included legitimization, identity, ethnicity, conflict resolution (as distinct from settlement) and others that did not fit into the traditional approach that dwelt on authoritarian structures and normative and coercive processes.

The conceptual notions that characterized the pre-World War III literature defined the areas of interest. They included a wide range of subjects from 'alienation', through 'management' to 'values' and 'violence', but as you will not have the opportunity to explore any pre-holocaust libraries it may be useful to summarize the position that had been reached by the 1980s.

A number of these conceptual notions formed sets. 'Legitimacy', 'law and order', 'coercion', 'obligation' and many others formed a set relating to 'authority'. However, to a significant extent the sets in which notions were placed reflected trends in thought and discourse. Depending upon pre-theories, notions can be in several different sets. For example, 'minority rights' can be in a set with 'authority' and 'majority rule', or, alternatively, in a set dominated by the notion of 'universal needs', depending on whether the enjoyment of rights is regarded as a cultural norm or a human requirement. Furthermore, a developed terminology is necessary to remove ambiguity. 'Rights' and 'needs' were sometimes used in the contemporary literature interchangeably. However, 'rights' were traditionally referred to within majority–minority constitutional relations, while 'needs' were more and more referred to in the literature as universal requirements.

Classification of conceptual notions (the logical process) and analysis of trends in the literature (the analytical process) suggests seven sets of concepts that seemed relevant to behaviour relations. In the historical order of their emergence they were:

(i) Authority.
(ii) Institutions and structures.
(iii) Responses to authority.
(iv) Individual and human needs and values.
(v) Growth and change.
(vi) Processes in dealing with conflictual relationships.

(vii) There began to emerge a seventh set of inter-disciplinary concepts despite the fact that no truly inter-disciplinary and multi-level literature had emerged. It did not seem possible for the one person—student or practitioner—to deal at the one time with all sets. The 'authority' set was concerned with law and order, the role of authorities, sanctions, norms, management. It was institutionally oriented. The people affected were members of the elite. The response literature dealt with reactions to authority. It was change oriented. The people affected were subjects and not members of the elite. There were some contributions that approximated to an inter-disciplinary status and in so doing provided the beginnings of another set—an inter-disciplinary set in which the whole of a topic was analysed, not just its parts. This developing literature was clearly different in kind from all others. It contained contributions that embraced assumptions and methodologies that were currently regarded as 'controversial'. For example, many authors moved freely from one level in society to another, assuming that the same behavioural patterns were common to all. It was not a large literature; but it was one that combined all the sets, including methodology, one that tended to focus on and to be stimulated by contemporary social and political events. What emerged from an analysis of the literature was how intellectually misleading were studies based on disciplines. Truman (1968) found it necessary to differentiate between behavioural science and political science. He tried to determine the impact of the former on the latter. What he found was that there are 'institutional' and 'behavioural' scientists, the former being involved in what turned out to be a remote type of applied science, tending to accept the current institutional constraints as part of the data. They pushed into the background the theoretical behavioural framework in which they were, as applied scientists, operating. This emerging seventh set, a behavioural set, included those who consciously endeavoured to integrate theoretical and applied knowledge.

These classifications are logical within a decision making system—stimulus, response, feedback, inter-action. They also accord with the contemporary developments in thought. Indeed, the literature in each category can be attributed its own time span. The trends in the literature show the successive developments that took place between one set and the next.

It was possible to obtain a general picture of these trends in writings by examining entries in the Library of Congress, which is unfortunately probably not available to you. Words such as 'ethnicity' and 'identity' loomed large in the titles of the acquisitions of the late 1970s whereas some years previously words such as 'power', 'roles' and 'law and order', dominated. For example, in the period from 1968 to 1973 there were nine book titles that included the word 'ethnicity' and 138 that included the word 'identity'. In the period between 1974 and 1980 there were 116 and 418 respectively. The British Museum similarly showed an increase: 'needs' jumped from 362 to 1381. A similar increase in interest in 'rights' and 'values' was evident.

Within this broad perspective of trends, it was possible to make a closer analysis of typical works. In all spheres scholars were more and more resting on assumptions that implied the probable existence of needs or wants that were universal. In 1977 Burns looked for the 'Wellsprings of political leadership' and found them in 'the vast pools of human energy known as wants, needs, aspirations and expectations'. Also in 1977 Sir Leslie Scarman asserted that 'there is a natural law springing from man's own humanity which must be incorporated into the positive law of the state'. Barrington Moore (1979), when trying to define the notion of justice, was driven to observe that 'it is obvious that human beings do have something that can be called innate needs'. He tentatively drew attention to non-physical needs such as needs for respect and recognition, for identity (which he called 'distinction'), for the absence of boredom or for stimulus, for control (which he related to freedom to be aggressive against dangerous targets). He concluded that:

> As a working hypothesis, I propose a conception of innate human nature, innate in the sense of being *prior* to any social influences but not necessarily immune to them, for which not only physical deprivations are noxious but also psychic ones; specifically, the absence of favourable human responses, boredom, and the inhibition of aggressions.

In the field of comparative politics Peretz (1978) argued in his contribution 'Universal Wants: A Deductive Framework for Comparative Analysis' that the future of comparative politics as a study rested on the assumption that there were some wants that were constant across political systems. The sociological literature on deviance was moving toward the same hypothesis. Box (1971), for example, argued that the explanation of deviance was found in the denial of needs such as identity, relationships, opportunities and expectations. Furthermore, interests and needs *will* be satisfied by one means or another, legal or illegal. Psychology was slow to shift from organizational to motivational explanations. Weiner (1979) somewhat reluctantly included in his wide-ranging review of approaches to human motivation a final chapter on 'Humanistic theory and personal constructs'. Psychology was greatly concerned with what Weiner terms 'crippled people', whereas the so-called humanist school, he suggested, studied 'healthy people'. In his review, however, he seemed not to have been aware of the type of psychological interest evidenced by non-psychology writings such as those referred to above. This reluctance of psychologists to break with tradition and the explanation of deviant behaviour within a normative law and order framework, which suggested that any individual who did not conform to social and legal norms was in some way crippled, was attacked by some controversial biologists. Wilson, who wrote a comprehensive review of biological literature in 1973, contributed a Preface to a book entitled *Sociobiology and Behaviour* by Barash (1977), in which he said:

> To understand evolutionary history and the contemporary biogram that it produced is to understand in a deeper manner the construction of human nature, to learn what we really are and not just what we hope we are, as viewed through the various prisms of our mythologies. Assisted by sociobiological analyses, a stronger social science might develop. An exciting collaboration between biologists and social scientists appears to have begun.

What these scholars were saying, in essence, was that organizational approaches had been too superficial. To argue, for example, that alienation was a function of private property, was not to give an explanation of alienation. Private property was a source of alienation only if the institution of private property frustrated some need, such as that of distributive justice, security and so on. Socialism, or the absence of private property, could contain sources of alienation no less severe (for example, the absence of participation and of a sense of control). As Scruton (1980) argued, 'if a factory labourer is compelled to view his activity as means, then this is so whether or not the final product lies in the hands of the individual, the collective, or the State'. Alienation occurs in any system if, in practice, participation and identity are denied. Smallness—in national groups, in industrial organization, in schools—could have pay-offs in human satisfactions that outweigh the claimed benefits of economies of scale and largeness.

Even those scholars who did not consciously adopt a needs approach and those who opposed it had to refer to it. Gurr had a book with the title *Why Men Rebel* (1979). He was referring to all men, at all times, in all societies. There was a strong implication in it that there were some basic human needs to be fulfilled. Weiner (1979) admitted that all individuals learn—it is a universal trait. Learning is an inherent and ontological part of human behaviour. In fact, as we will see, those who succeeded best in defining in precise terms what human needs were, adopted a learning framework: the needs defined were those that are fundamental to the process of learning. They are deduced from the process of learning.

It is noticeable that the writers mentioned above were not using methods based on statistics or probability theory. The existence, display and use of these needs were not a statistical phenomenon. All individuals had them. This purported to be a natural law as conceived by natural scientists. To quote Wilson again:

The purpose of sociobiology ... is to develop general laws of the evolution and biology of social behaviour, which might then be extended in a disinterested manner to the study of human beings.... The evidence is very strong that there does exist a human biogram, a pattern of potentials built into the heredity of the species as a whole.

In short, there appeared to be a persistent trend over a long period of time from a focus on institutions to one on persons and groups; from organizational explanations to behavioural explanations; from the study of overt behaviour to the study of covert behaviour; from ideology to empirically based testing of theory. Twentieth-century experience had persuaded writers that the individual might be an independent variable, that there might be no institutional devices, rule-governed norms or organizational influences that could contain the ontological propensities of the individual. Generalizations, explanations and predictions were possible once universal patterns of behaviour were discovered. Behavioural science was, in these circumstances, no different from natural science. Both had the same universality, both were governed by empirically observable patterns of behaviour, both required at some level of analysis hypotheses concerning the unobservable reasons for overt behaviour and these required experiment and testing. If Winch were correct in his claim that there could be no science of behaviour, in which mode would biology be: natural or social science? The reality was that we were living in one world, not in two so sharply separated in kind that they were not subject to the same processes of analysis.

Human needs and control theory

At this point we should define the individual to which reference was being made, as distinct from economic, legal, psychological, organizational or ideological 'man'. In particular, the needs to which reference was made should be specified.

There remained little agreement on terminology when reference was made to the universal variables. Needs, wants and values were sometimes used interchangeably. Pirages (1976) distinguished needs from wants: 'Basic human needs are physiologically determined while wants are socially determined'. As already quoted, Barrington Moore (1979) made a similar distinction: 'specifically, the absence of favourable human responses, boredom, and the inhibition of aggressions'. Burns (1977) in trying to define the role of leadership, used the terms 'needs' and 'wants' in the opposite senses; but the attempt to differentiate was clear.

The needs to which many social scientists were drawing attention could not be determined by examining the overt behaviour of the individual. This would lead only to labelling: aggression, frustration, violence, anti-social behaviour and other terms were descriptions of behaviour that could be seen and had no explanatory power. As already indicated, non-visible behaviour and needs must be specified by a deductive process. If learning and social development require consistency in response, security, identity and recognition and if human behaviour is characterized by learning and social development, then humans pursue consistency in response, security, identity and recognition as part of their learning process. It is reasonable, further, to argue that organisms have a genetic drive to learn, for existence depends upon learning, despite frustrations in the environment. These learning needs *will* be fulfilled. If recognition, identity of self and some measure of control over the environment are human needs, then the absence of these conditions will either be overcome or abnormality in behaviour will develop as an adjustment to the adverse conditions.

It is in this area that Sites (1973) made his main contribution:

We have demonstrated the emergence of eight needs in the individual: a need for response, a need for security, a need for recognition, a need for stimulation, a need for distributive justice, a need for meaning, a need to be seen as rational (and for rationality itself), and a need to control. The relationship among these various needs is extremely complex. The last four needs emerge because the first four, which emerge out of the necessary dynamics of the socialization process, are not and cannot be immediately and consistently satisfied.

This quotation, however, does not do justice to the insights that led to the assertion of these eight 'needs'. 'Control theory', which Sites advanced, provided a synthesis of organizational and coercion theories, on the one hand, and of behavioural theories on the other.

Sites argued that the concept of power was indispensable to all existing theories of social and political behaviour. He attempted to synthesize apparently contending theories around the notion of control. His initial proposition was that if individuals and groups attempt to control their environments, there must be a reason. He further hypothesized that the reason was to obtain gratification of needs, including the need for self-realization.

The needs which he hypothesized stand outside any particular society: they are universal and genetically related to the individual. This is not to say that the individual and group would not use the cultural and other norms of their society to gratify their needs.

Needs theory had an acknowledged history. Sites referred to Ardney (1966), Maslow (1954), Thomas (1923) and Fromm (1955). In addition to those cited above all had their own lists of needs. What was striking was the similarity in all these lists.

Sites freely admitted that human needs were no more visible than the atom and its particles; but that this should not prevent social and political scientists from working with the concept any more than it daunted physicists. His belief, based on anthropological and other studies, was that the influence of individual needs was 'many times stronger than the influence of the social forces which play upon man'. So strong were these influences that 'individuals step out of the "real" world into a world of their own in an attempt to find fulfilment of more basic needs or at least to escape their complete frustration'. The individual's most fundamental drive was, in his view, to attempt to control his environment in order to meet his needs. Society never completely conquers the individual. Culture must be viewed as a continuous creation or re-creation—a gap always existing between human needs and the interests and values of power elites.

It followed that, in this view, the individual uses the norms of society as tools to the extent that they are useful in the pursuit of human needs. If they are not useful more appropriate ones are invented; as Sites said: '. . . if needs cannot be met by being honest, the individual tries something else'.

Control theory was wide-ranging. Such a framework provided at least some explanation of the behaviour of under-privileged delinquent gang members, middle-class adolescents who experienced a sense of lack of control by themselves over their lives, revolutionaries who were those awakened to the possibility of a changed society but who had no opportunities of participation in the decision making processes of society.

It is interesting that control theory could be deduced from simple and non-controversial propositions relating to learning and development: the early socialization process—rewards and punishments—conditions infants (people) to behave in certain ways. Parents (authorities) are no less required to behave consistently if their conditioning is to be effective. Thus infants (people) and parents (authorities) are engaged in a reciprocal process. The ability to control responses becomes the dynamics of social life. Thus it could be inferred that there are certain social conditions necessary for growth and development, such as consistency of response, stimulation, security and recognition or approval. In addition, in social life, distributive justice, meaning, rationality and control could be essential to development and socialization.

From such a theory, much could be deduced that is of social and political significance to the pre-World War III world. (If the theory of universal human needs is valid, these observations will apply to whatever society emerges.) As Sites argued, there was here a potential explanation of a great deal of 'deviance' at all social levels. It followed that, once the individual was adopted as the unit of analysis or explanation, there were objectively determined guides to policy—bases on which goals and policies could be assessed and predictions made as to success or self-defeating consequences.

Box (1971), who dealt more specifically with 'deviance', adopted the same approach. In his view 'social structures may be "legitimized" or "institutionalized" for only a minority of the members of that system'. Deviant behaviour was nothing less or more than rule breaking: only some people, sometimes, could satisfy their needs within the framework of the law. For him it was a matter of surprise that there was not more 'deviant' behaviour—he asked the question, 'Why don't we all break the law?' His answer was not deterrence, but values attached to relationships. Most individuals establish social bonds, 'the remainder of the population are free to engage in delinquent behaviour'.

Control theory was an explanation of 'normal', ordinary, conforming behaviour. There was the 'abnormal' aspect. For example, there is frequently over-reaction in human behaviour in the sense that the motivation is not the normal pursuit of needs satisfaction. A child or communal group deprived of rewarding relationships, recognition, security and identity over long periods will tend to perceive injustice and deprivation and be aggressive even in circumstances that do not require this. This is a matter of political significance. Political and social leadership, conforming and non-conforming, has tended to attract such individuals. Control and power for its own sake was not a part of control theory as such: but such a theory demonstrated how 'aggression' could be created by circumstances, thus pointing to the long-term costs and consequences of needs deprivation.

An assessment of control theory

We have been discussing trends in the behavioural sciences, the experiences of those engaged in research and consultation and the hypotheses to which they were led. What emerges is a hypothesis that asserted the existence of specific human needs that have a bearing on social organization.

There was, over the ages, a continuous development in political thought; but this development involved many different opinions, particularly on the process of development of society and the reasons for various aspects of human behaviour. At the time when people were first aware of their socio-political conditions and gave thought to them, the Natural Law explanations of society and of the behavioural patterns of members of communities seemed reasonable: human organization was believed to be God-given in the sense that it emerged naturally out of evolving kinship and face-to-face communities in which role was unambiguous and a coercive framework irrelevant. Any sanctions were those imposed by tradition and by nature. An organizational–behavioural debate was irrelevant to that kind of society. Socialized behaviour and natural behaviour were as one. With the emergence of larger and more complex societies, there was a differentiation of power through the normal processes of social exchange in such a wider society. New roles, authoritative roles, specializations and classes emerged. Positive Law, reflecting elite interests, inevitably dominated. Its consequences for others were mediated to some degree by the need to legitimize it by reference to Natural Law and principles of justice. The instrument employed was organized religion which claimed its Canon Law to have natural roots. The organizational–behavioural conflict, accompanied by its self-interested ideologies, set the stage for contending approaches and adversary institutions in which contending interest groups came face-to-face (D'Entreves, 1970). In twentieth-century industrial society the application of Positive Law began to require such an extent of coercion that both it and the law-enforcement authorities were challenged, especially in developed societies. Socialism, which sought to remove the conflict of interests out of which Positive Law developed, had been able to do no more than to create yet another interest group or class and its own Positive Law that was no less under challenge. Human needs were frustrated on a large scale in all societies and the more law and order was enforced to control frustration the more the frustration. A widespread concern about the legitimacy of even the most liberal and apparently legitimate authorities developed, and the individual once again emerged as the focus of attention and the unit of analysis. 'The rich kids' of Switzerland who rioted in the 1980s, the members of protest movements of many kinds and the terrorists who sprung from relatively privileged classes, were demonstrating that there were features of societies, of all political types, unacceptable to a significant number of the units that compose them.

Roberts (1979), a lawyer who developed an interest in anthropology, reviewed trends in the investigation of social control processes. He pointed out that the scientific interest in natural processes as an explanation of behaviour had its origins in early legal studies, subsequently given the title of anthropological law. Sir Henry Maine wrote *Ancient Law* in 1861. In it he traced the way in which human civilizations passed through various stages of development in social organization with an evolving system of law-making from the stage at which there was nothing more than the ordinary controls that apply in any small kinship group to the most complex of laws in a developed society. At about the same time others in America and Western Europe were pursuing the same question. The notion of a 'primitive law' was widespread and the interest in it was of concern because of the increasingly coercive elements in developed societies. In 1924 Rivers (in his book *Social Organization*) took the view that where there was group sentiment there was no need for any definite processes of law making and enforcement. In 1926 Malinowski wanted to know how societies held together 'without courts and police', and a few years later Radcliffe-Brown was interested in the formulation of law as 'social control through systematic application of the force of politically organized society'.

These studies showed how there was a tension between concepts of law, implying some element of Positive Law, and sociological concepts of control, implying something akin to Natural Law. The end result seemed to be a synthesis reflected in an interest in the notion of processes. Conflict was perceived as a normal and inevitable feature of social life, to be explained in sociological terms. The perception of control was as in traditional societies, quite different from the law-based notions of classical theory. Settlements were seen to be based on problem solving processes rather than on the zero-sum or win-lose outcomes that occurred under the common law model. 'No-fault' approaches that developed, especially in the United States, and community means of handling deviance as developed, for example, in Ohio (see *Time* magazine, 1980) reflected this growing realization that there was an interaction between the norms of society and the requirements of the individual that could not be resolved by coercion in favour of social structures and institutions. Positive Law, accompanied by a high level of enforcement, was being seen, in retrospect, as a diversion, be it a persistent one, from the main stream of development of processes that cater for the interests and requirements of the unit members of societies. The interest in the individual as the independent unit focused attention on the lack of legitimacy of pre-World War III societies, the way in which elite norms had prevented the changes needed for cultural norms to reflect individual interests. It gave some insights into why class societies, including those societies that had bureaucratic classes, were inherently unstable.

This was a historical argument: the way in which the essential nature of man had pervaded thought and perceptions of society as it had grown in size and complexity. The individual emerged as the independent variable despite a persistent belief that the individual adapts to and is socialized into social organizations and social norms. The same conclusion could have been deduced from *The Logic of Collective Action*, to use Olson's (1965) title. The idea that a person, seeking to maximize his/her cost benefits, acts in accord with social norms on the grounds that through this his/her individual interests will best be satisfied, which is the argument on which classical theory heavily rested, could not be sustained. The individual unit, person or group, would pursue his/her self-interest regardless of the social interest, in any set of conditions in which needs can be satisfied best in this way. As Box (1971) observed, the relevant question is not why some persons did not conform, but why all persons did not find it in their interests not to conform. He thought that if identity or recognition were needs and if, in practice, the norms of society were useful tools in fulfilling these needs, then the norms would be observed. If not, they might still be observed; but only because of values attached to relationships within the society. In the absence of such relationships there was no cost benefit reason for believing that observance of a group common interest would promote an individual interest. The employee could usually gain the benefits of unionism without being a member and without the cost of fees. He/she would become a member and pay the costs if there were, in addition to gains to be achieved, valued relationships with other employees. Value attached to relationships was the essence of recognition of legitimized leadership, loyalties, nationalism, altruism, social conformity and other attitudes that lead to social integration, co-operation and self-restraint despite self-interest. Structural explanations of behaviour assume that, and were valid only when values were attached to relationships within society. They fell apart when there were no such relationships.

In this sense there was a return to the individual as the independent variable, a return to the basic tenets of Natural Law. The individual was, clearly, never out of the picture entirely. Marxists, following a classical tradition, always claimed that the essence of humanity was in free creative activity, in full and free expression and development. Marx, quite deliberately, it seems, made a clear distinction between 'alienation' and 'estrangement'. Alienation, especially alienation at the work place, was his preoccupation because of changing industrial conditions. However, the term did not explain the human response. Clearly there could be alienation due to social and political conditions, for instance the absence of participation and of a sense of control and the absence of identity for minorities, just to give two examples. Marx was well aware of this ontological element. 'Estrangement' was his term to apply to conditions that affected biological human nature (Wallimann, 1981). Positive Law found its legitimization in the common good through which the individual would benefit most. But the means were organizational and in the circumstances structure inevitably reflected class and not necessarily common-good interests. The 1980s return to the individual as the unit of analysis was far more in accord with the Natural Law notion; but it was a return to Natural Law in a scientific age. The reference point was no longer some vague notion of natural justice based on some mysterious God-given social norms. It was based on needs that ranged from the physical to the behavioural. These had to be met if the unit within the social system were not to be malfunctioning and destructive of society and itself. The organizational–behavioural debate was being resolved by a synthesis, by a focus on the individual unit to the extent that the needs of this unit determined the effective operation of the social system of which it was part. The goal was the Positive Law goal of a harmonious society in which the unit adapted to the changing environmental conditions, but within the limits set by the satisfaction of human needs. The means of this interaction between changing conditions and the requirements of the units within society were the Natural Law processes by which organizations and political systems were adapted to the evolved and evolving needs of the participants. What a pity there was this gap between such insightful knowledge and the goals and policies you pursued both at home and abroad.

THE LETTER

The Consensus of Assumptions

We considered we lived in a scientific age. We measured and used computers to sort out data. We tried to be precise in the use of terms, though this was difficult because we were not always clear on the notions the terms or symbols were intended to represent: what was 'power', 'legitimacy', 'justice'?

Because we were so conscious of the need to be scientific, we tended to argue that a hypothesis was a personal matter, the scientific interest was in testing. Now we know that this was rubbish: the personal hypotheses of politicians and administrators were 'tested' in disaster! A hypothesis is of great practical and scientific interest: it is from this starting point that propositions, theories and policies are deduced.

Hypothesis forming rests on a long and intense process of experience and thought and, in particular, the questioning of assumptions. Usually assumptions are hidden from us: we accept past traditions so easily, we are so much bound by culture, that we tend not to question conventional wisdom. In retrospect, we were particularly bad at questioning our assumptions, bad at being scientific about hypotheses. Many, if not most, of the important ones which we took for granted have now been proved to be false. You will have been alerted to this in the last section. It signalled a radical change in that it was based on the view that the individual is the unit of explanation of social and political phenomena, not structures. This is a departure from tradition—and the consequences are far-reaching. It throws into doubt much of our traditional and consensual thinking about political relations.

There is no point in discussing all the traditional assumptions that were found to be false. Once you have a few examples you will be able to think about many others: you will find that almost all your thought processes and all the policies that led to disaster, were even then open to challenge.

Integration

Let us start with the assumption, which was an inherent part of traditional thought, that societies are integrated social and political units and that, if they are not, it is the task of authorities to make them so. This was assumed to be the case throughout the history of thought, probably because when social organizations were first developed they were small traditional societies not far removed from tribal groupings in which shared values led to coherence; in feudal societies high levels of coercion brought about the same result. When political units increased in size and the authorities needed to maintain internal and external security, it was convenient to maintain social and political cohesion and integration as an ideal and as a strategy. However, with the development of multi-ethnic societies, including many different interest and cultural groupings, there was no justification for making this assumption. On the contrary, societies had coherence, in as far as they did, despite the absence of shared values and despite coercion which was usually self-defeating. This coherence was necessary because of transactions and cross-cutting affiliations, which were not greatly different from the processes that operated between nations. Attempts to integrate them, attempts to deny identity to minority groups, attempts to impose authoritative norms, led to conflict and to disintegration. There was an extensive literature on this subject, there were the 'coercion' theorists and the 'shared value' theorists, each trying to explain social coherence or integration; neither considered the possibility that what they were trying to explain did not exist in multi-ethnic and industrial class societies.

The significance of a false assumption is in its implications. Arising out of this assumption there were others, necessarily false if the integration one were false. The notion that democracy was rule by the majority arose out of this assumption. It was a useful notion in small groups in which there were shared values. However, it had no relevance to situations in which there were minorities that themselves had shared values different from those of the majority and which, for this reason, suffered discrimination at the hands of majorities. In the 1960s the Greek Cypriot majority based its argument for a unified constitution on this idea of majority rule. Only after great losses did it realize that it had been mistaken and that it was necessary to accept the claim by the Turkish minority that it had certain identity and recognition values that had to be met. In Northern Ireland the British Government defined the activities of the Catholic para-militaries as rebellion and, as such, it had to be suppressed by force. Unlike in the Rhodesian situation they refused to talk to the 'terrorists': it was a majority–minority situation in which the minority was expected, subject to certain safeguards, to agree to majority decisions.

Legitimacy

Closely related to the assumption of social and political coherence is the notion of legitimacy. You will recall that in the years that led to World War II and, indeed, one of the triggering reasons for the war, was the existence of many governments that were 'legal' because they were internationally recognized and in effective control, but had no 'legitimacy'. Understandably, the distinction was not usually made. The majority of the governments that were members of the United Nations had no legitimized status. To survive they relied on external support and on internal repression. A legitimized authority is one that derives its authority from those over whom it exercises it: it is self-sustaining in this sense. This type of authority is best conceptualized as 'role differentiation'. In a small meeting someone, for the convenience of all, is asked to act in the role of chairperson. Authority is merely one of many roles that are played by units within a society, carrying no more and no less importance than any other. A legitimized authority requires no coercive support.

There are many conclusions to be drawn from this. There are positive advantages in smallness of political units. There are advantages in decentralization and regional autonomy. There are disadvantages in integration used in the sense of federation. You will recall the many abortive attempts at this kind of integration in South East Asia and in West and East Africa. The European Economic Community (EEC) was a prime example of dysfunctional integration. Functional co-operation between separate political units, just as functional interactions between individuals in the same system, are useful; but structures that take decision making away from members of political systems are dysfunctional.

There was a curious ambivalence about this in the past. There were those who claimed to be progressive and forward-looking who advocated wider political units such as the EEC, on the grounds that this was a move toward 'one world'. If you were sophisticated you were on the side of more and more integration! Integration, as we now realize, was a structural approach that denied the behavioural needs of human organization: it was far from sophisticated.

Adversary systems

A related notion was that to be 'democratic' it was necessary to have adversary systems, government and opposition, prosecution and defence. As you know this led to a lack of continuity of policies and waste of experienced people. There could never be analysis of situations, there were inevitably adversary debates and stances to maintain one position or another regardless of considered interests. People became very cynical about party politics and politicians who played the party politics game.

The adversary notion crept into international politics:

whatever one side suggested or did had to be attacked by the other as a trick or interpreted as malign. You may well ask what was the alternative? The West, in particular, had been so accustomed to the adversary party political system that those of you who are from the West will be puzzled as to what can take the place of adversary politics. Yet within Western societies there were many institutions that were analytical and problem solving. Generally speaking there was a more positive approach to decision making within small groups— a question of shared values, probably. However, it was not just a question of shared values. The judicial system was adversary; but departures from this were more and more frequent as the 'no fault' approach developed. Juvenile crime was often dealt with by the relevant people getting around a table and trying to find the best solution. Even at the political level, behind the scenes in committees, it was possible to be analytical outside an adversary framework. It could be argued that where there are class differences and contending interests, adversary systems are inevitable. It could also be argued that adversary systems consolidate and promote group differences.

Boulding (1970) was interesting on these matters. He was very critical of the dialectic approach: being scientific, in his view, was to take the best from different systems. The West could well have adopted some of the consultative processes of the 'socialist' States, or at least tried to understand and to interpret accurately what they were trying to do within what was virtually a one-party system. The socialist States never managed to bridge the gulf between rulers and the ruled; but there were the seeds there of something that should have been watched with interest and studied objectively.

Zero-sum conflict

The adversary system rested on an assumption that relationships were win-lose or zero-sum. The gain of the one was the loss of the other. If one party won the other lost, if one interest group won, the other lost. This was how conflicts of interest were perceived. In practice both lost because of the way in which the conflicts were fought out. In industry employers and employees lost as a result of strikes. There were often win–win solutions; but these were not perceived or revealed because of the adversary, bargaining processes. In practice, conflicts are rarely, if ever, of this zero–sum character. They are usually over resources that are not in short supply, such as identity and recognition. The tactics, the question of who occupies what position, may be zero-sum, not the achievement of goals. Look back at the pre-World War III situation, were there no positive sum outcomes possible? Was a balance in favour of the West, which affronted the East so much, a tactic or a goal? It was merely a tactic and an unwise one if the goal were war prevention.

Related to this there are many other assumptions, that conflict is over 'objective differences of interest', that settlement of conflict and not resolution is the only means. Mitchell wrote a useful book about these matters in 1981. There was not a great demand for it at the time, despite a clear and most important exposition, because the West, for whom it was written, was so steeped in adversary politics and the related processes and assumptions.

Negotiation

There has always been an assumption that in a power politics world bargaining and negotiation, leading to 'settlement', are the appropriate techniques by which to resolve conflicts.

A study group was set up in 1963 by the David Davies Memorial Institute for International Studies to examine the peaceful settlement of international disputes. Its membership ensured a serious and thoughtful analysis and the views expressed represented conventional wisdom and informed opinion on this subject. The striking feature of the report was the way in which the group was pulled in two different directions. On the one hand, confidence in judicial processes was affirmed and reaffirmed; on the other, there was a realistic acknowledgement that they had failed. They argued that there was nothing fundamentally inadequate in judicial procedures; the problem was a lack of willingness on the part of States to submit to voluntary or compulsory third-party determinations. At the same time the group acknowledged the particular difficulties associated with traditional means of peaceful settlement, in particular, the existence of the general problem of freedom of action that was likely to persist and which inhibited States from accepting not only judicial processes but even less formal ones.

In development from judicial settlement to mediation and conciliation, there is a continuous weakening of the decision making role of the third party. The development of these 'weaker forms' of intervention represented a historical as well as a behavioural development: the League concentrated on judicial and arbitral processes, the United Nations far more on less formal ones. While in practice it is difficult to assess relative success, there is reason to believe that the less formal the technique the greater the range of application and the greater the success. Whether this be so or not, there is a presumption that each successive process was introduced because of the failure of a previous one.

Some international lawyers assumed that the progression was not because experience supported the use of less formal procedures, but because States were *unwilling* to accept the more formal ones that allowed third parties to influence conditions of settlement. This legal reaction begged the main question: if States were unwilling to adopt judicial and formal procedures that took decision making away from them, then these procedures were irrelevant to the circumstances. It was pointless to grumble about the condition of world society and blame States for the lack of success of some techniques. The intellectual difficulties experienced in considering traditional means of peaceful settlement of disputes could not be overcome by impressing upon States their moral obligation to fall in with behavioural patterns suggested by intellectuals and idealists. The reality was that both judicial procedures and the less formal processes of mediation or third-party interventions were incompatible with the nature and operations of international and, indeed, with many aspects of municipal society.

Techniques for the resolution of conflict must reflect the needs of the people concerned. Procedures that present the conflict as a zero-sum game in which the gain of one party is the loss of the other, cannot lead to a decision that satisfies all parties. Judicial processes were of this kind. Arbitration and conciliation and, indeed, even more informal procedures such as bilateral bargaining and negotiation, postulated that bargains and compromises were desirable and possible and that external pressures could help to make them acceptable. Such postulates have no support in behavioural studies. The independent decision making role of States in world society was more jealously defended than in most behavioural relationships. The techniques failed because their objective was settlement by third-party decision making or by compromises that did not fully satisfy the felt needs and aspirations of all parties.

Deterrence

Finally, in this set of examples of false assumptions, let us look at one on which we have based political and social organization: the assumption that threat and coercion deter.

Deterrence strategies, which were the main means by which major Powers endeavoured to control their power rivalries, had been shown by past wars not to be an effective instrument. Indeed, they probably had built into them processes of escalation that rendered them self-defeating. The reasons why they failed were becoming clearer even in the early 1980s, even before some of you started to talk, not about deterrence, but about 'winning'.

Threat of punishment, threat of costs greater than satisfactions to be gained, has an influence on the decisions of individuals and groups. The rules of the road and parking rules are obeyed in many cases because of threat. Often a deliberate costing is undergone; sometimes there is a calculated preference for a fine or cost that is less costly than the gains to be made from defiance of the law in particular circumstances. It might be that some crimes are deterred by deterrents more costly than any gains, subject to calculations as to the risks of being caught and the level of punishment. For the most part crime is not deterred—most crime is probably not even discovered. Can we deduce from this that societies are as harmonious as they are because of threats and deterrents: is coercion a significant explanation of social order?

At first it seems as though the assumption that threat deters is axiomatic, and it has been fundamental to our notions of social organization and law and order. When in practice deterrence fails it must be argued, on the basis of this view, that this is merely because the amount of deterrence and coercion and risk of detection are less than required or that some different form of deterrence and detection is needed. No other explanation of the failure of coercion to contain deviance is possible within the framework of classical theory: to recognize the failure of deterrence as a control instrument would jeopardize a whole set of conventional notions involving rights, obligations, morality, values, the socialization process and the justice of institutions and legal processes.

So much was it an accepted assumption that threat deters that writers focused mainly on its processes (for example, how threats could be made more effective by ensuring credibility, by promoting accurate perceptions of threat and by maintaining a sensible relationship between crime and punishment). Other studies that accepted deterrence as an effective instrument of control just as fully, focused on the relationship between levels of punishment and degrees of risk in being apprehended. Rarely was the effectiveness of deterrence seriously questioned. Yet the empirical evidence in crime statistics—and wars—suggested strongly that threat did not deter.

The assumption that threat deters was clearly articulated at the strategic level. National defence strategy was merely a special case of the belief that adequate negative sanctions prevent the 'rational' decision maker being 'aggressive'. Officials in the North Atlantic Treaty Organization (NATO) argued in the 1980s that if it had not been for NATO there would have been aggression in Europe from the East. Warsaw Pact officials probably used a similar argument. 'How do you know?' was regarded as an irrelevant or unnecessary question. In practice there could not be an answer because there could not be a test. Now we know!

In the pre-nuclear age the empirical evidence was clearly that strategic balances and military threats did not deter 'aggression'. There was no evidence that the nuclear threat was any more of a deterrent than was the mighty power of the United States against Japan when the latter bombed Pearl Harbour. The failure of capital punishment as a deterrent to those engaged in organized fighting and killing in a communal conflict would suggest that 'rational behaviour' included in some circumstances the acceptance of the risk of paying the highest possible price—which means that there was no deterrent. On these purely formal and logical grounds the assumption needed to be questioned whether deterrence was, in any but the most trivial circumstances, an effective control mechanism.

The effective control of behaviour is not coercion by

authorities to observe the law or morality, but as control theory argues, a value attached to relationships which would be threatened by antisocial (legal or illegal) behaviour. It is interaction with parents that leads the child to conform because whatever other satisfactions he/she may seek, he/she experiences satisfactions from his/her continuing relationships with his/her parents. So it is throughout social life: the observance of etiquette and social norms is a direct response to interactions and affiliations. In due course, the consequent behavioural patterns become habits and are internalized, so that conforming behaviour frequently continues even in the absence of rewarding satisfactions or unrewarding disapproval. It follows that if people are denied the opportunity to interact, they have less incentive to conform and fewer opportunities to learn the required behaviour. Thus the child, deprived of a relationship with a parent, a teacher, a peer group or authorities—or the adult or the nation similarly deprived—cannot be expected to conform to social norms. The original reason for the deprivation may be that there is no parent or substitute parent, for some reason no link with the parent, no relationship with the teacher because of poor performance or a personality clash, no links with authorities and society for some environmental reasons or maybe because the person concerned is retarded, physically handicapped or rejected on racial or religious grounds. In every case, there is an absence of positive or negative inducements relating to the maintenance and development of relationships—effectively, an absence of relationships—and, therefore, an absence of self-imposed control because there is no motivation for it; there is no value attached to any authority.

The two factors, the absence of relationships that, if present, would promote conformity and the presence of pressures that motivate deviance, together ensure an increasing level of organized crime, for relationships can be developed within a criminal subculture, thus satisfying a basic human need. The norms of this subculture are policed, as in the wider society, by the value its members attach to relationships within it. Thus all its members are required to observe norms, such as violence against the wider society from which they feel rejected.

Having thus deviated, having not observed the norms of society, the person is required, on the basis of classical theory, to experience a form of negative sanction. Punishment, even physical punishment, by a parent is usually in the context of a relationship. It is not the physical hurt that has effect. Within a system of relationships, physical or any other punishment is a means of communicating disapproval. What is at stake is the relationship and to preserve this the child is prepared to conform if necessary. Etiquette must be most unimportant to a small child, as is unselfishness; but if relationships can be secured by conformity, then some degree of self-discipline is worthwhile. However, punishment by a parent, teacher or authority with whom there is no valued relationship rests entirely on the physical pain or the deprivation inflicted, with which the human organism has a physical and mental capacity to cope. It is this form of punishment, unassociated with valued relationships, that the courts, authorities and society inflict. Behaviour is not altered by it in the direction intended: on the contrary, the behavioural response is to damage the person or property of that parent, teacher, authority or society as soon as opportunity offers. Furthermore, the form of punishment is usually exclusion from society and, more seriously, from the few kinship and other relationships which remain.

This is an important matter in solving social and political problems. Threat and deterrence are subject to limited boundaries of effectiveness, being relevant only in relation to the daily rules of social relationships that rest on mutual convenience, such as the rules of the road. They have only marginal relevance for behaviour that is destructive of social harmony (for example violence against the person, corruption, exploitation, robbery, revolt, etc.). The degree of social harmony that societies do experience is due mostly to different influences, such as values attached to day-to-day relationships. Because this is the case, quite fundamental changes are required in the explanation of harmonious social relationships and in policies designed to promote these. Not even the most ideal social system you can imagine can avoid a measure of disharmony due to structural and institutional constraints on behaviour; but unless attention is given to values attached to relationships, it is likely that deviant behaviour may be more pronounced than need be the case and punishment of deviance more likely to increase than to decrease it.

This reasoning is applicable to the inter-State level. In a Great Power rivalry the tendency was to isolate, to withhold recognition, to resist parity, to withold technology and needed supplies as threat or punishment. As was the case with Japan when it entered World War II, ultimately there is nothing to be gained and everything to be lost by observing the norms of international society if these threaten some important national interest. The ending of *détente* undermined any influences imposed by deterrent strategies. When the Soviet Union and the United States were seen to be experiencing both internal problems that would take time to resolve and external problems in their spheres of interest, this should have led to co-operative responses. However, in fact it led to war.

What I have been trying to convey here is that everything is open to discussion in post-World War III planning or in war prevention. If we do not discuss the problems, our policies will lead back to holocaust. This does not mean that we should adopt indecisive, stop–go policies or endless debates. What we must do is get the original hypothesis right, the definition of the situation from which policies flow. This is not necessarily a time-consuming process: it is an attitude of mind, an ability to question and to entertain new ideas and altered perspectives. This, in turn, implies appropriate decision making institutions, ones that promote discussions and do not drive people into defensive positions. However, let us now test the value of such exploratory attitudes by looking at industrial relations and then at political relations.

Needs Theory Applied to Industry

The previous section may seem a little remote to you: does (or did) needs-bonding theory, which is what control theory is all about, have a practical application? Your concern will be primarily with relations between nations or different survival groups; but let us take, as an application of needs theory, industrial relations as you knew them. Let us hope that they do not re-emerge in the pre-World War III form!

The problem area of conflict in business, as in wider social and political organizations, was located in authority relationships. We–they authoritative relationships were part of the Western tradition and were clearly implied in classical theory. Political, judicial, industrial and other social institutions were predominantly adversary—government and opposition, prosecutor and defendant, employer and employee. There were decision making concepts and models that reflected this traditional approach to authoritative relationships. They were reactive and power-dominated models, as adversary relations must be. Unfortunately, even socialist countries did not succeed in eliminating we–they authoritative relationships.

In the 1930s there was a strong tendency to tackle such relationships by advocating changed structures, more egalitarian systems. But experience and thought soon suggested that changed structures would not eliminate the problem: there have to be leadership and authorities no matter what the political system. You will find that it is always within the decision making process, not in structures, that there is the source of conflictual problems. The decision making process itself determines options available and outcomes. Reactive hierarchical processes have conflictual consequences. They are usually legal but not 'legitimized'. By the employment of coercion they make puzzles out of problems, they give rise to coercive settlements and not to resolutions of conflict. Decision making that is effective is inter-active; it is a process that comprehends all likely responses before decisions are taken. An adequate theory of behaviour would point to likely responses. Behavioural theory based on human needs that *will* be pursued by the individual regardless of constraints—such needs as identity, recognition, control and stimulus—was a better framework in which to understand and to manage pre-World War III industrial relations than classical power theory. In practice inadequate theory about human needs has to be supplemented by the participation of those concerned in a non-bargaining and problem-solving process designed to bring these needs to the surface. This problem-solving process is quite different from what was traditional bargaining and negotiation. The role of the third party is quite different from that of the traditional mediator, as I will later argue.

These assertions arise directly out of the 'post-behavioural revolution' (Easton, 1969) that signalled a paradigm shift from a classically based interest in institutions to a concern with the individual as a unit of analysis to which we referred in the last section. This shift was not occasioned by a sentimental or humanist interest in the individual, but by an empirically based jolt: harmonious social organizations seemed to require an acknowledgement of the needs and roles of the individual. The focus on individual needs and on the negative consequence of their frustration was a feature of a wide literature, as we have seen. Philosophers provided the link with classical thought (Bay, 1958). Students of jurisprudence, for so long wedded to classical authority notions, began to take stock (Bodenheimer, 1971). Political scientists moved from a tacit recognition of some universal behavioural motivations (Gurr, 1969) to a more precise assertion of human needs (Zetterbaum, 1977; Burns, 1977; Davis, 1979; Parry, 1969). Sociology moved in the same direction (Box, 1971). Social psychology (Knutson, 1973) and anthropology added an empirical dimension (Enloe 1973). Indeed, there was a flood of works reflecting this new interest in human values. In the late 1970s it was coming together in general theories, which cut across disciplines and systems levels (Gurr *et al*., 1977; Burton, 1979).

Accompanying this post-behavioural revolution and causally related to it, was a revolution in methodology. Inductive processes, including case studies, had characterized industrial relations studies. They tended to be self-fulfilling: what was assumed to be the position tended to be confirmed by observation. They were giving place, as we will see in a later section, to deductive approaches in which theoretical behavioural propositions were examined and tested at different system levels.

Classical thought and post-behavioural reactions

In the 1960s and 1970s there was an apparent erosion of authority at all social levels—in family relationships, in the school, in the law and order area, in industry, in relationships between authorities and minorities and at the inter-State level. At each level the problems were analysed separately in separate disciplines. Different attempts were made to manage or to control existing structures and relationships—with the same lack of success. In retrospect, it seems that societies cannot be integrated by socialization and coercion, that deterrence has strict limits of effectiveness, that minorities will not accept majority rule, that small States do not accept the international norms evolved by Great Powers (remember Iran?). Generalizing, it could be asserted that traditional hierarchical authority structures are not viable. Industry is no exception.

It was widely argued in the decades just before World War III that this problem of authority relations, especially as applied to industry, could be dealt with only by fundamental changes in economic systems, that capitalism and the associated class system were the root cause of the problem. Certainly there would seem to have been good reasons, in many cases, for attributing friction between authorities and others to the existence of class antagonisms, to the existence of highly privileged minorities in societies, to the tensions between those who owned property from which they derived financial benefits and those who had only their labour to contribute to their earning capacity. While such gross inequalities as existed, both in incomes and in opportunities, must have prejudiced relationships, the view that capitalism and class relations were the source of conflict was not a sufficient explanation of the problems. Similar problems occurred within nationalized industries, within socialist systems, indeed wherever there were authority relationships. The problem appears to have been much deeper than one that can be defined in terms of particular 'isms' or structures. It appears to have been related to processes and to procedures more than to structures.

In dismissing structure as a major factor, I do not imply that there should not be structural change. Other 'isms' will develop—capitalism, socialism and communism were not the end of the line. You will—hopefully—invent a new 'ism', the nature of which should emerge in this letter. What you need to ensure, whether in relation to industry or to the wider society, is that whatever 'ism' does emerge does so as the result of analysis and of deliberately stated goals and not as the result of accident, a negative reaction to conditions, some ideological commitment or some pressure from narrow interest groups. Ideally, the new 'ism', the new system, should emerge by design and as a result of an understanding of the problems being experienced. The decision making process itself should, ideally, be capable of effecting radical changes both in structure and in process. The alternative is undirected violent change from time to time as systems outlive their relevance.

In response to the apparent failure of traditional institutions of authority at all levels of society to promote harmonious and orderly relationships, there was a fundamental, even revolutionary, shift in thought about relationships with authorities. We had not, at the point of catastrophe, fully realized the implications of this shift, the explanations of conflict that were implied and the policies that seemed logically to follow.

The problems inherent in authority relations had been debated over the centuries. The classical view was that there were those who had a right to expect obedience and those who had a moral obligation to comply. In this view authorities had a legitimate coercive power, which could be employed when socialization and moral sanctions failed (Lloyd, 1964). The philosophy underlying this view was that it was in the interests of the individual that he/she should be so coerced into behaving according to the law, for it was in his/her interests that society would be orderly and stable. Change would take place within the framework of institutions established by these laws. That these laws were necessarily elitist and authoritarian was not questioned. On the contrary, it was part of classical thought that there could be revolt and revolution in conditions in which such laws were seen to be incompatible with the interests of the society. Violence was acknowledged as an acceptable means of change.

THE LETTER

Authority relationships in industry were relatively new because industry with its large and organized workforce was a new development. However, decision making in industry inevitably conformed to these classical and traditional theories. The assumption persisted that there were rights and duties of the same order, that this was the nature of organization and management, that the alternative would be anarchy. This is a view most of you will have held. There was some democratization of decision making, as you recall, through processes of consultation with employees. However, the we–they relationship persisted. The superficial symbols of this relationship were for all to see: dress, times of work, means of salary payment, separate facilities, fringe benefits and others. The less conspicuous reality behind these superficial symbols was management power that came to the fore whenever there was any disagreement. This management power was part of the psychological environment of employees. Relationships in industry were merely an extension, as made necessary by technological changes, of relationships experienced under slavery, serfdom, feudalism and paternalism. The we–they structure appeared to be unchanged except in the relative power of the parties in the relationship.

Accompanying this approach to industrial relations there was the general political environment created by the 'we' interests. Non-Labour governments tended to stress the value they attached to incentives and strove to reduce taxes, which meant, of course, less expenditure on education, health and other social services—with widespread unemployment as a consequence. Especially in societies like that in the United Kingdom, the we–they relationship which characterized industrial relationships reflected a class relationship. However, the same attitude was as strongly ingrained in American thinking, though it took a less conspicuously class form. It was strongly believed that there were those who worked and won and those who did not. The view was that social provisions should not be such as to hinder those who were achievers or to make things too easy for those who were not. In both cases there was an assumption that there were equal opportunities for all—which in any society is a myth and in a multi-racial society is a hypocrisy.

The shift that was taking place in all the various disciplines concerned—philosophy, jurisprudence, sociology, politics, biology and others—was characterized by a decreasing interest in and importance attached to institutional values and a marked increase in and importance attached to human values. These latter were treated as though they were acquired or cultural values. However, as we have seen, they were being increasingly seen to be universal human values that exist in all social organizations. They were the fundamental requirements of the individual if there were to be social harmony. The concern was still with stable societies; but the means to this end were being perceived far less in institutional controls and far more in the establishment of conditions which make the individual an effective and cooperative member of the social system (Sites, 1973; Box, 1971; Burton, 1979).

One implication in this shift in thinking was in relation to leadership. In 1977 Burns had made a major contribution to understanding of the role of leadership and his starting point was 'the vast pool of human energy known as wants, needs, aspirations and expectations'. The distinction he made between 'power wielders' and leaders was useful. In his view legitimacy of leadership stemmed from the capacity of leaders 'to establish an authentic relationship with the genuine needs of followers'.

The implication of this emerging theory was that material interests were far less important than had been traditionally thought. This was of particular importance in industry where it had been assumed that the main goal of workers and unions was increased wages. Wage bargaining, according to this system of thought, was likely to neglect other concerns and was a compensation for a loss of identity, security and control. Increased wages would not bring industrial peace.

However, there was a much wider and more important implication. If conflict were not primarily over material values, then the problem was not the division of a cake of a given size. Conflict related to social goods that were not in short supply. National and international security was in infinite supply—the more one party experienced the more others experienced. So with these other non-material values such as participation, identity and recognition: once tactics, defence strategies, bargaining positions, were differentiated from goals and once the goals themselves were discussed, then, it was discovered, parties had common goals that were mutually supportive. This meant that bargaining was irrelevant. The appropriate response was a problem solving one, where goals were analysed in depth and the options explored by which they could be achieved without bargain or compromise (Kelman, 1972; Burton, 1969; Mitchell, 1981). We will be dealing with problem solving in a later section.

Let us re-state this shift in thinking and its applied implications. Power is the ability not to have to adjust to change, to prevent change, to impose burdens of adjustment on others. In traditional theory there were those who had rights to expect obedience, to expect (moral) obligations to obey. In such a coercive framework there was no need to consider the values and responses of others. At all levels authorities had a right and even a duty to enforce the rule of law by deterrents and punishments. Acquisition of power became a goal because it provided the means of authoritative control. The only means of change was revolution.

Later, power theory was shown to have internal inconsistencies and to lead to self-defeating policies. Its place was being taken—too late—by 'control theory' which subsumed aspects of power theory. Power theory and control theory both asserted that the unit (individual or nation) adopts all possible means, including alliances with others, to promote interests and needs. Power theory held that coercion and deterrence were the means of control and that these required power. Control theory, on the other hand, acknowledged certain needs that were universal and which could permanently be frustrated by coercion and deterrence. Such needs *would* be pursued, no matter what the constraints (a phenomenon you have now perceived at the inter-State level). Consequently, the mechanisms for attaining goals had to be such that they would not be self-defeating by reason of the responses from others who no less sought to attain the same goals. Hence, control theory invited consideration of behavioural responses of all kinds, whereas power theory was uninterested in behavioural responses, which, it was assumed, could be suppressed.

The policy processes that logically flowed from these two theories were no less fundamentally different. Power theory gave rise to bargaining and the traditional types of peaceful 'settlement' of disputes, courts, mediation and conciliation. Control theory gave rise to an analytical and exploratory, non-judgemental and non-coercive exercise, with a view to arriving at an agreed 'resolution'. The former was a reactive exercise of coercion based on an assumption that conflict was due to differences of material interests and was, therefore, win–lose or zero–sum. The latter was a problem-solving process based on an assumption that conflict was due to threats to non-material values commonly held. These were not scarce products, but social goods that increased in availability the more they were experienced.

Re-active decision making

Let us first consider traditional decision making theory and its models. The decision making process with which you as administrators are familiar, evolved out of classical theory and its underlying philosophy. It was conceived as a vertical process. Commands, coming down from the apex of the decision making pyramid, which was comprised of a small elite, were applied to the mass of people below who had the obligation to obey. In so far as there was any protest response communicated upwards, it was dealt with within the power framework that this structure implied, at least to the extent that available power made this possible.

The traditional idea, put forward initially by Modelski (1962), was that of a simple input–output system. The inputs were the power inputs, resources, etc., that were available to decision makers. The outputs were the distributions of the available power made by decision makers. It was clearly an elitist model: the assumption was that there were in any organization those whose job it was to supply the resource and those whose job it was to make allocations according to their goals and interests. It was for this reason that politics was defined as 'the authoritative allocation of values' (Easton, 1965). In this model the actual decision making process was not represented: it was not even conceptualized. The concern was only with the supply of inputs and the allocation of outputs: given power and authority the actual process of allocation was assumed not to present difficulties. The model drawn by Modelski makes no provision for the decision making process as such (see Figure 1).

By the late 1950s, however, it was widely appreciated that the decision making process itself was the important part: how inputs were recorded, processed, assessed, filed, retrieved and so on (Deutsch, 1963). More and more complex models of the decision making process emerged and systems analysis helped to promote these considerations. The input or stimulus and the output or response featured less largely in conceptual thinking. The visual models drew attention to processes

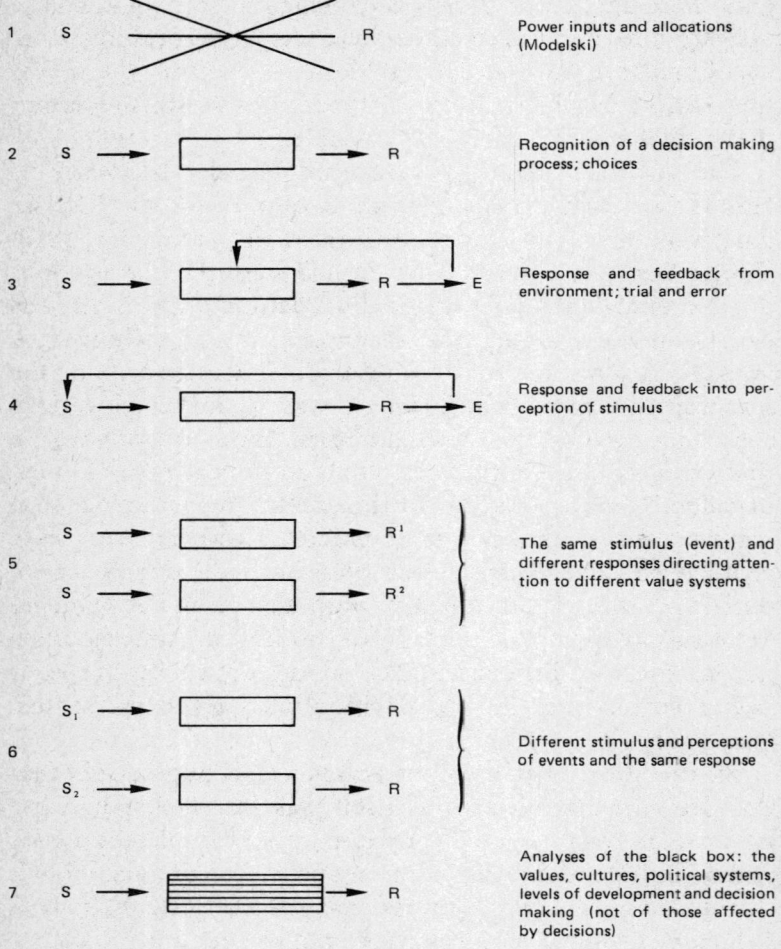

Figure 1: Reactive decision making models

that were thought to take place within the 'black box' of decision making.

More and more complications were inserted as experience and awareness directed attention to other details. The cybernetic or feedback process loomed large after the invention of electronic self-steering and self-correcting devices (such as were introduced into aircraft) provided models on which cybernetic thought could be based. Further complexities were, in due course, introduced to take account of the experience that different stimuli sometimes produced the same response in different systems and different responses were sometimes produced by the same stimulus of different systems. Values, motivations generally, were taken into account.

However, all of these models, from the simplest stimulus response to the most complicated decision making process, had in common those features that had been inherited from classical tradition. They all depicted reactive processes and they all assumed a major power element in decision making. They did not deal with values and motivations of those affected by decisions. They were, in short, all models of elite responses to environmental conditions and to changes in these conditions. The assumptions that there were rights to expect obedience and moral obligations to obey were implicit in all. All were in a framework in which it was assumed that interests were in conflict, that those interests were primarily material, that relative power determined outcomes and that power bargaining was the relevant decision making process.

By the 1980s we had come to the end of the line with these models. No matter how sophisticated, they did not seem to be helping us to solve authority problems in the wider society or in industry.

Situation definitions

Decision making processes themselves limit options and determine in advance the range of outcomes that are possible.

Courts make judgements within the boundaries of the law: they cannot arrive at decisions that they think just if that decision is against the law. Mediation seeks compromise: the mediator tries to obtain a half-way argument. Bargaining confines negotiation to a set of proposals, the outcome being likely to reflect the bargaining power of the contestants.

The invention and the selection of these processes reflect definitions of the problem in advance of knowledge of it. A communal conflict, such as in Northern Ireland, occurring in a democracy in which minorities were supposed to accept majority rule, was defined as rebellion. Police and military coercion was the appropriate remedy on the basis of this definition. The facts that there were identity and recognition issues, that there was evidence of discrimination against the minority, that the minority had no effective voice in decision making, were given little weight—even though these influences in practice proved more powerful than military coercion.

The invention of processes, their selection in particular cases and the definition given to particular situations, arose out of assumptions made about the behaviour of persons and the role of authorities. These were not assumptions held just by a few people or only by decision makers. They were the consensus of the views held by members of society generally—as you know. They were inherent in Western traditional thought and philosophy. There were many of these assumptions, as we have seen: relationships in conflict were 'win-lose'; States were or should be integrated units; institutional and social values were more important to the preservation of societies than were human values.

What we were seeking—and what you will now have to seek—were processes that did not prejudice or limit outcomes in advance of a wide and deep knowledge of the situation, in advance of the discovery of possible outcomes based on adequate analysis and of adequate definitions and valid assumptions. These are processes that do not limit, in advance, discoverable options. In short, what we sought—and what you must now seek—were realistic definitions of situations, from which would flow policies. Definition is the end-product of analysis, not the beginning.

In the more traditional authoritarian system it was expedient and efficient to employ power and coercion as a means of ensuring discipline and compliance. Countervailing behavioural pressures were curbed, at least temporarily. This made puzzles out of problems.

A puzzle has a known outcome, as a simple mathematical 'problem', a maze, or a technical puzzle. A problem, on the other hand, has many possible outcomes, many leading to new problems. No final and definitive answers are possible. The strong and understandable tendency in decision making was to make puzzles out of problems. There was a need for certainty, for decisive leadership, for firm agreements. Where there was an effective power capability, complex behavioural and organizational problems could be simplified into puzzles: decisions could be enforced. In the short term this was regarded as effective and positive decision making. In the longer term there were almost always adverse effects. Important variables had been suppressed. Decision making that is effective takes into account all behavioural variables, regardless of the complexities in analysis and in procedures.

Legitimacy in authority roles

Wherever in human societies there is an erosion of authority, where there are management problems that are characterized by resistance, then—by definition—there is a legitimacy problem. In classical and traditional theories authority and leadership were derived from tradition, legality and charisma or some combination of these. In all cases they were concerned with we-they relationships. Legality was defined pragmatically, by reference to recognition and effective control.

There is in social organization, however, a distinction to be made (as I have already suggested) between that which is legal or legitimate and that which is legitimized. Legitimized authority is that which is self-supporting, because it is derived from those over whom it is exercised. There is no implied coercion or manipulation necessary. While there can never be a pure form of legitimization, any more than there can be of any ideal type, it is possible to observe and to make judgements about relative legitimization. There were, as you recall, many authorities represented at the United Nations that were legal, but had little legitimization. Once this distinction is made then a fourth source of authority is revealed; this is role differentiation. Legitimized role differentiation is a familiar concept when applied to labour specialization. It was never applied so directly in relation to political authority and leadership roles. An obvious example of legitimized role differentiation is the part played by the chairperson at the meetings you will be having (I hope) to discuss this letter. It is possible to conceive and to model an inter-active political decision making process that had this legitimized foundation.

Inter-active models of decision making

Instead of a reactive power model of decision making, such as has been described above, let us now consider an inter-active model. Essentially it is a stimulus–response model; but there is an inter-action between all parties that make decisions or are affected by decisions in any particular situation.

Such a model implies a set of assumptions that are distinctively different from those that underlie classical authority relationships. They include the assumption that conflicts of interest, while appearing to the parties to be zero–sum, are usually not so, perhaps never so, once perceptions, value hierarchies and costing have been analysed and explored;

that there are processes that transform what appear to be win-lose conflicts into positive-sum ones; that there is a distinctive difference between settlement and resolution; that non-adversary type decision making in institutions opens up options not available to traditional adversary type courts, parliaments and industrial institutions of decision making (Burton, 1969).

Looking at decision making from this point of view, there are three sets of models. There are those that make puzzles out of problems—those that are within a coercive framework. Second, there are those that recognize the need to satisfy legitimate aspirations; but at the same time finally rest on power or a compromise that reflects relative power. The third set is of those that are problem solving in the sense that they rest on analysis and seek outcomes that are positive-sum, satisfying the values of all parties. This last set relies, as is argued below, on a third party that is non-judgemental, non-directive, non-manipulative and that seeks only to ensure an effective inter-action between parties.

In Figure 2, three examples are given in the set 'Complexities ignored: puzzles'. They are effectively reactive models such as have been described above. The first is a straight coercive model of the stimulus-response type, taking no account of the responses of other parties. The second is one in which there is an element of trial and error or cybernetic decision making in which the more powerful concedes something. The third is one in which the powerful party endeavours to take into account some of the needs of others in a paternalistic mode. These reactive models are given merely to show the limits of such decision making notions: within a power and reactive framework, this is the limit beyond which reactive models cannot go. This was the point reached before World War III by many authorities in politics and in industry: there appeared to be no further step that

Model No.	Puzzle or Problems	Model	Pay-offs	Description	Dynamics
1	Complexities ignored: puzzles	A → Perception of situation → Power → A's goal	$A = +x$ $B = -x$ where $x = 1$	Reactive Power model: win-lose outcome	A determines outcome (e.g. war or compulsion) *Settlement enforced.*
2	Complexities ignored: puzzles	A → Trial and error cybernetics → A's goal	$A = +x$ $B = -x$ where $x > 0.5$	Win-lose, but in less extreme proportions	A influences outcomes having experienced B's responses. *Settlement enforced.*
3	Complexities ignored: puzzles	A → Analysis of many complexities in relations from ascendancy viewpoint → A's goal	$A \sim B$ (interdeterminate)	Paternalistic model	A influences outcome and takes into account B's goals. *Settlement enforced.*
4	Transition	A → As above from A's position ↕ Direct negotiation ↕ B → As above from B's position → A's goal / B's goal	Stalemate or $A = +x$ $B = -x$ where $x > 0.5$	Perceived incompatible goals; but recognition that relationships are based on relative power and both sides must participate in decision making	A cannot determine outcome and must compromise. *Settlement agreed.*

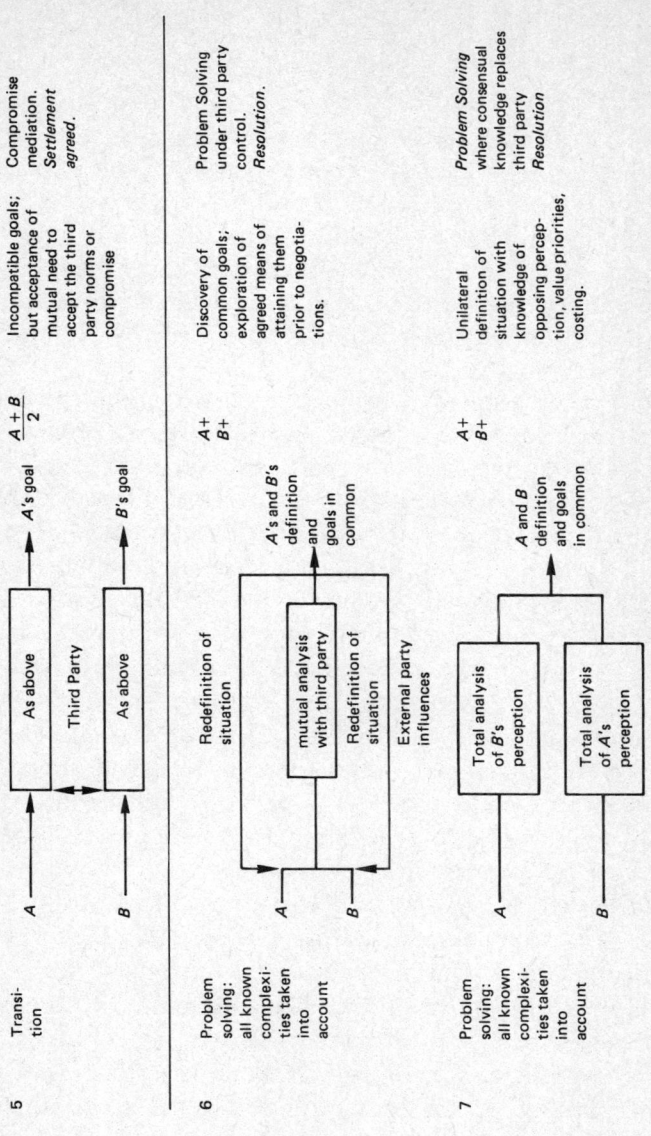

Figure 2: Inter-active or problem solving modes. A is a powerful State in inter-State relations or a central authority or an industry in industrial relations. B is a weak State, minority or organized group

could be taken within the philosophies and conceptions that were at the base of reactive notions of authority.

The second set, 'Transition', in which there are two models, shows the transition from coercion to problem solving. It depicts direct negotiation with other parties, but still within a power framework. Alternatively there is third-party mediation introduced to assist negotiation. In both cases the outcome is likely to be compromise, neither party being satisfied, with potential conflict written into the settlement. However, it is an advance on what is possible within a purely reactive model.

The third set 'Problem solving: all known complexities taken into account' is the interesting one. Here there are two models, one in which a third party enacts a role to assist in problem solving—a special role not to be confused with arbitration or mediation and which is discussed later. The other is a somewhat unrealistic and idealistic model, yet a logical extension, which assumes that the parties themselves have the professional knowledge of a third party in a problem solving context and have the willingness and ability to apply that knowledge to their own situation. It is not wholly unrealistic or idealistic. If there were an adequate theory of behaviour and if there were a widespread understanding and knowledge of it, parties could work out their relationships without the assistance of a professional third party. However, parties to disputes usually have no widespread knowledge of such a theory and, indeed, no such theory. There are appropriate islands of theory of which you will be aware. This is why a professional third-party role is possible: a great deal of theoretical behavioural knowledge is a common possession. We return to this when we consider the notion of problem solving and the role of a third party. This section was merely to draw attention to the application of needs theory to decision making in industry.

THE LETTER

Needs Theory Applied to Political Relations

We have taken the relatively simple case of industrial relations to see what relevance a needs theory has to conflict resolution. Now let us look at political relations. The questions we are asking are 'Which is the better theoretical explanation of political relations?', 'Which is the better base on which to make predictions?' and 'Which is the better base on which to formulate and to assess policies, traditional power theories or behavioural explanations?'

If this appears to be an abstract question we can translate it into practical terms. Which was the better explanation of Japanese and German behaviour in relation to World War II, the more recent Northern Ireland problem, the Middle East conflicts, Cyprus fighting, Soviet Union–United States relations, Vietnam—the explanation that rested on power, its acquisition and employment and the needs of the State or the explanation that took into account ethnicity, identity, recognition and other such behavioural motivations?

In a later section it will become clear that my colleagues at the Centre for Analysis of Conflict and I were not ivory tower academics. We used to get our hands and reputations dirty by leaving our books and becoming directly involved in actual conflicts such as Cyprus and the 'confrontation' of Indonesia and Malaya. This is not the occasion to report in detail on these excursions and, in any event, reports are already available (Burton, 1969). As an example of the different approach, including resistances to it, I wish to dwell on Northern Ireland.

Between 1969 and 1976 I visited Northern Ireland frequently and regularly, initially at the invitation of the Northern Ireland Community Relations Commission—a most useful and important organization that the British Government abolished. During these visits I was in direct contact with the para-militaries from each side, traditional politicians, the officers commanding the army and the Northern Ireland Office. I made notes of every interview. I wish I could share these with you. They are too long and too personal for publication. They are also shocking. They reveal in stark detail how the British Ministry of Defence took control of Northern Ireland primarily in order to ensure there was no settlement. The typical worst-case-analysis mentality of defence officials feared the emergence of an independent Northern Ireland, which would put British and NATO defence strategies in jeopardy. Remember how the West tried to prevent Cyprus becoming genuinely independent? You would be amazed at the lengths the Defence Departments and the Northern Ireland Office (headed by a Defence Department official who subsequently went back to the Defence Department) went to ensure that the two para-militaires would have no opportunity to come together with a view to working out a future.

In 1974 the British Government set up the 'Gardiner Committee'. The mandate was to advise on what provisions and powers in addition to those already existing should be taken to deal with terrorism and subversion. I wrote a submission to this Committee. It is a long while ago and in it are parts not relevant now; but it draws out the difference between a power and a problem-solving approach, based on different definitions of the situation. I have decided to give you the full and unamended text:

Submission to Gardiner Committee
1. The Committee has been asked by the Secretary of State to consider provisions and powers required to deal with terrorism and subversion. It is submitted:
(i) that there are provisions and policies that could lead to an early and effective end of terrorism and subversion, and to the establishment of general harmony within Northern Ireland society (para 12);
(ii) that in so far as 'provisions and powers' in the terms of reference by the Secretary of State refer to coercive or repressive action, these

THE LETTER

terms reflect assumptions about the nature of terrorism and subversion in Northern Ireland which may not now be valid (para 5);

(iii) that such provisions and powers for the suppression of terrorism and subversion in Northern Ireland are likely now to be self-defeating in that they will create violence (paras 6–10); and

(iv) that such provisions and powers are likely also to be self-fulfilling, in that the violence so created will be argued as proof of the needs for them (para 11).

2. The evidence on which these submissions are argued has been obtained deductively from studies of conflict at different social levels, and empirically by studies of other similar communal conflicts, such as Cyprus; by discussions separately and together with leaders of the opposing factions who have been and continue to be those described as terrorists and subversive; and by discussion with the Director and members of the staff of the Community Relations Commission who, over the years of current conflict, have been closely associated with the problem and the factions primarily involved.

3. The Director of the Community Relations Commission and some members of his staff have read and discussed these submissions and are in general and particular agreement with them. These submissions have not been discussed with the leaders of the opposing factions in the Northern Ireland conflict, but it is believed that they reflect generally their view-points.

4. A detailed analysis of the Northern Ireland problem has not been presented in making these submissions. It needs to be acknowledged, however, that each assertion that there is a need for provisions to suppress terrorism and subversion, and any alternative proposal, rests on a particular definition of the problem. Just as the terms of reference of the Secretary of State reflect an attitude and a definition of the problem (see para 5 below) so do any proposals for dealing with the situation. It would therefore be relevant to these submissions to make such an analysis; one has not been made merely for reasons of length. If the following submissions seem to challenge officially and conventionally held view-points and policies, then a request for a verbal or written analysis would be welcomed. Suffice it to argue at this stage that, as Weber observed, there is an inverse correlation between the level of policing and enforcement necessary in a society, and the level of legitimacy of its authorities. The legitimacy of Stormont has been challenged. The legitimacy of the para-military authorities of both sides, and in particular of those who challenged the authority of

Stormont, has also been called into question by the Secretary of State and by the Prime Minister. In the view of a large section of the Northern Ireland community the levels of legitimacy of the Army, and of the Northern Ireland Office, the two agents of Westminster, would seem to be low. The following submissions rest on the general thesis that the Northern Ireland problem, like the problem of terrorism and subversion generally, relates to the legitimacy of authority, and that additional provisions and powers given to an authority that already lacks legitimacy cannot succeed in promoting peaceful relationships —on the contrary. Short of total suppression of civil liberties and human rights, including massive internment, terrorism and subversion can be eliminated only by dealing with the problem as it is perceived by the parties involved.

5. *The Terms of Reference.* The committee's terms of reference imply that there is a phenomenon of terrorism and subversion that exists without due cause, that can and should be suppressed, and that enforcement actions can in some way solve the existing problems of conflictual relationships. Such a view arises out of many unstated hypotheses:

(i) that 'law and order' can be defined in classical terms, that is a set of norms to which authorities expect obedience as of right, and to which those over whom authority is exercised are obliged to conform. However, the classical notion referred to the individual in relation to authorities and did not deal with majority-minority relationships in which there are ethnical, cultural and other identifications which create permanent and substantial minorities. Furthermore, this conception of law and order implies that simple majorities within a party political structure attract legitimacy, even when minorities may not effectively be represented;

(ii) that there are effective alternatives to violence in such situations, such that grievances can be overcome by constitutional means. The classical and traditional notion, and one reflected even in the UN Charter, is that violence is justified in defence but not as a means of change. However, the contemporary notion of 'structural violence' suggests that overt violence is a response to violence imposed by structures; the source of conflict is in existing structures. There appear to be few opportunities to alter structures, even discriminatory ones, by peaceful means where these structures are defended by law and the 'legitimate' violence of authorities;

(iii) that violence and subversion are perpetuated only by a minority of violent and probably unbalanced men and women. However, empirically it is now clear that the structural violence in Northern Ireland is perceived by a large proportion of the population, many of whom are prepared to react outside the law. Violence has become as natural a response as fighting a national war or being a soldier engaged in repressing violence. Anyone who had had the opportunity to meet with the so-called 'extremists' on both sides in Northern Ireland—and in other situations—finds that they constitute a body of dedicated leaders, who act as they do because of their deep commitment to communal values. Two Secretaries of State have been impressed by the personalities of 'gunmen' and 'extremists' on the few occasions on which they communicated face to face. They, like Nyerere, Makarios, Nkrumah and others who were 'subversives' prior to being acknowledged leaders, see their role as the protectors of communal values. They are typically sensitive and warm persons who resent the fact that they are forced by structural circumstances to enact their role. They have no less difficulty in sorting out their value systems than Quakers and other highly motivated people in Britain did in the First and Second World Wars. These same people, because of their motivations, are the first to take initiatives to explore options and to end conflict, where often political actors tend to maintain stances. This has already been shown to be the case in Northern Ireland, as is indicated in para 7 below. Provisions and powers to deal with terrorism and subversion that do not exploit this common feature of communal conflict, and which seek, on the contrary, to restrict the freedom of movement of effective leaders, is likely to be destructive of peaceful relations between the communities they represent.

6. *Suppression is self-defeating*. In practice the Army has acted on the set of hypotheses reflected in the Secretary of State's terms of reference, and has accordingly carried out searches, organised informers, and escalated internment. It has been assumed that law and order can be maintained by suppression, pending a political settlement. There is evidence that, at least in the current circumstances (see para 11 below) the acts of suppression themselves are now a major source of violence. This is a view held by both 'extremist' parties, and also by members of various political parties.

7. The current circumstances which have created these conditions seem not to be widely known and understood. This is in part because there have been behind-the-scene developments that could not be reported freely, and in part because events tend to be interpreted within a particular perspective; but more importantly because some of

these developments and opportunities for peaceful relations have seemed to be in conflict with the immediate and longer-term interests of the Army and of the Northern Ireland Office (see paras 9 and 10). Whatever might have been the nature of the conflict between Protestant and Catholic communities in the past, the strike organised by the Protestant Workers' Council, in association with the para-military groups, led to a redefinition of the situation by both sides. This strike was a reaction to the Sunningdale proposals that included a political relationship with the Republic. In practice this 'extremist' reaction led to moderation and a desire for conciliation. Experience in organising the strike led para-military leaders to think in political terms. They had to cater for the needs of Catholic minorities in their midst, they had to take political decisions, they had the opportunity to assess the personal and political motivations of their traditional political leaders and they did not like what they perceived. After the strike, aware of their political power, they had to think out their position, consider what, if any, initiatives they should take about the situation in general, and how from their new position of strength they could come to terms with the Catholic minority. They sought advice regarding political solutions. The barrier appeared to them to be the constitutional demands that the opposing IRA appeared to seek. It was suggested to them that the position might not be unlike the Cyprus one in which leadership of each side was forced by circumstances to adopt public stances regarding Enosis and double-Enosis, while wishing independence and local identity. This was privately confirmed by the IRA leadership who 'were moving in the direction' of discussion on the basis of existing boundaries. In the circumstances it was decided to convene a three-day conference of members of the Workers' Council and para-military groups, and this led, despite reported statements to the contrary, to a series of direct talks between the two sides. These established certain common interests, common problems and some agreements on controlling violence.

8. These discussions signalled altered policies by the Army and the Northern Ireland Office, to encourage and make possible discussion within and between communities. Both were kept informed. However, both apparently saw dangers in these developments. The Army maintained the need to continue searches and internment, and its role in Northern Ireland which it values: 'it could not be pushed out'. The Northern Ireland Office argued that 'wider implications' had to be taken into account, by which was probably meant that these discussions could move in the direction of an independent Northern Ireland,

which itself has wider security and strategic implications. A suggested initiative by the Community Relations Commission to convene a conference of relevant persons was discouraged by the Northern Ireland Office on the grounds that it 'could not be controlled'.

9. The Army had been responsible for copying and releasing to the press the confidential agenda of the three-day conference, including proposals for discussions with the IRA, thus embarrassing the leadership of the Protestant para-military groups. It continued searches and internment just at the point of time when relaxation seemed desirable, and indeed after the statement by the Secretary of State of 24 June 1974 saying he welcomed discussions, and after the White Paper of 4 July 1974 calling for open discussions. An agreement made on 11 July between the opposing parties to take appropriate steps to stop 'car bombs' and 'sectarian murders' was reported to the Army, but a series of arrests followed before the agreement was ratified, whereas releases were indicated as being the means to encourage peaceful relations. As was anticipated by the opposing parties, there was reaction to these policies and after five days some bombing recommenced. In practice the presence of the Army, the need to defend themselves by using informers, and the practice of searching (and, it is widely believed, 'planting' evidence) contributes to violence against authorities, and also violence within communities when informers are sought out and punished. In the post-strike situation, the conflict moved away from Catholic v. Protestant towards a growing confrontation with authority by both groups. The policies of the Army have been in this sense, self-defeating.

10. The policies of the Northern Ireland Office were no less self-defeating in so far as it appeared to be cultivating traditional politicians —'the elected representatives'—in a situation in which altered political alignments had made them less relevant, and in so far as it was discouraging discussion between emerging political factions and the Secretary of State, or even discussions among these new factions. The fear among para-military leaders of a return to the status quo ante the strike, including domination by formerly established politicians each representing a particular sectarian or nationalist position, led to a sense of alienation from the Westminster Government and the Northern Ireland Office in particular. This was accentuated when the White Paper called for elections to a consultative assembly, but in the absence of freedom of movement and of discussion—a set of conditions which would favour the traditional alignments and parties.

11. *Suppression is self-fulfilling.* The leaders of the main para-military groups respect the ability of each other 'to deliver the goods'; but both acknowledge that without evidence that the end of violence has direct pay-offs in terms of the end of searching and internment, and positive steps toward consultation between the communities, they cannot maintain an effective leadership toward their common goals. Both fear that their attempts to promote a dialogue could provoke a reaction that they could not control if some minor breakdown in peaceful relations occurred in the absence of progress toward their goals. The Cyprus example is pertinent. There the two communities were living side-by-side, their two leaders were in constant discussion; but an attempted coup on one side re-created the communal fears and bitterness. Were this to happen in Northern Ireland, the Army would claim it as evidence of the continued need for repression. Indeed, increased violence followed a short pause in car bombing during July; but this was a self-fulfilling consequence of the refusal of the Army to respond to the new situation, and not evidence of the need for further internments.

12. *Positive Proposals.* There are provisions and policies that could lead to an early and effective end to terrorism and subversion. The credibility of these rests on the attitudes and values of the conflicting factions, and on the general analysis of the situation, neither of which, as already noted, are here detailed.

(i) The role of the Army needs to be confined strictly to the sophisticated, highly disciplined and professional role of peace-keeping as developed by the United Nations, in which there is meticulous avoidance of police action, and which is confined to acting as a buffer between the two communities, and as a third party, as and when violence makes this necessary. It is suggested that the pay-offs to the Army would be greater in that such experience is likely to be more valuable in the future than the type of military exercise in which it is now engaged, and would no less create the valued conditions of comradeship.

(iii) Both para-military groups acknowledge the need for adequate unarmed policing in their areas, especially now that stable leadership is diminished with internment, and with the increase in civilian crime due to years of tension and disturbance. Both would agree that unarmed RUC police could be acceptable provided there were a Watch Committee set up in each area to which any complaint of partiality could be referred. If adequate police forces were not available either or both of two procedures could be introduced: (i) the withdrawal of the Army from test areas in both communities and the substitution of police, and/or (ii) the introduction on loan of British Commonwealth police—from Australia, Canada and New Zealand—many of whom are of Irish descent and who have had experience in communal situations such as Cyprus.

(iii) As a matter of urgency the internment problem needs to be tackled thoughtfully so as to release quickly many valuable community leaders, and many who have been interned without having, to the best knowledge of the para-military organisations, been engaged in any violence or illegal activities, and to identify those who have committed civil crimes and need medical help. (Interviews conducted in prison revealed several disturbing confusions between ordinary civil crime and communally motivated behaviour.) In terms of law all have committed a crime. In terms of danger to society on release, there is need for differentiation. This would require a well-chosen committee of persons who could examine each case and take advice from community leaders and community workers who know the persons and circumstances.

(iv) Freedom of movement needs to be established so that there can be meaningful discussion of policies within and between factions. At present it is not possible for the para-military Catholic factions adequately to discuss political alternatives among themselves. To make discussion effective, an organisation needs to be created which has a clear mandate to initiate and to promote discussion in the spirit of the White Paper.

(v) Elections to a constitutional assembly should not take place until new alignments and ideas are explored, and this is a process that could take a year or more. It is a general principle that no such constitution should be drafted without reference to actual relationships. Nor should one be drafted by a body controlled by party political alignments. A constitution needs to reflect what is evolving. In the meantime, a nominated executive with powers to advise the Secretary of State on the basis of unanimity, needs to be appointed: a group of 20–25 persons drawn from the main factions in conflict and from general interest groups. The unanimity procedure would ensure problem-solving discussions, rather than power bargaining and debate. This would have the effect of making unnecessary the Northern Ireland Office which is perceived as an alien body.

(vi) The issue of independence should not be avoided. The referendum which gave a choice between Dublin or Westminster, Sunningdale, which seemed to imply some assocation with the Republic, and official discouragement of open discussion among the factions involved, were all presumably dictated by a desire to ensure that there could not be an independent Northern Ireland. The independence issue is not one Britain should fear if discussed openly. But any attempt to contrive an outcome, such as the Constitution which Makarios finally rejected in Cyprus, will be self-defeating.

13. *Conclusion.* The Northern Ireland conflict presents a problem, not merely to Westminster, but more especially to those most directly involved in the two communities. 'Provisions and powers' seems to suggest a policy of repressing conflict by coercive means, whereas what are required are policies, provisions and powers designed to assist the communities in resolving the problem. In practice the communities, primarily through their para-military leadership (which is usually the case in such conflicts), are moving in this direction; but this is despite both the security and the political policies of Westminster.

Northern Ireland has been taken merely as an example. The point to be made is that traditional power explanations, theories and policies failed. East–West, North–South, the Middle East, spheres of interest, attempts at integration, deterrence, the handling of minority problems—failure all along the line. Why? There was something inherently wrong with traditional coercive policies. Perhaps control theory is not the final answer, almost certainly it is not. However, it incorporates previous theories including power theories. It is an advance in terms of our increased experience and knowledge. The lesson is that we have to be prepared to innovate, to re-think, to move away from the traditional, to explore—and the exploration of the behavioural seems to be the most exciting and the most rewarding. After all, the problems we are talking about are, in the last analysis, the problems of satisfying the needs of the unit members of societies, people.

How to Reason

We should pause here. I have argued that thought by the 1980s was undergoing radical change in the face of failures and of increasingly serious political and social problems, that human needs were coming to the fore as the explanatory or independent variable.

This change is not wholly explicable in the absence of some reference to no less remarkable changes that were taking place in how to reason.

'How to reason' placed in the middle of a discussion of war avoidance might seem a little irrelevant to you, as administrators do not have time for such philosophical or ivory tower pursuits! I want to urge on you the view that this must be the starting point of policy formulation. As I said in the Introduction, get this wrong and you will get the lot wrong. The wrong hypothesis, the wrong first definition of a situation, leads to false policies, usually to self-defeating ones. I keep harping on the Northern Ireland example: defined as a minority rebellion in a democracy, there was only one logical policy, repression, coercion, punishment, official violence; defined as a majority–minority problem in which ethnicity, identity, recognition issues were important, the remedies were quite different. Many of our widely held pre-World War III assumptions were false. Many of our working hypotheses were guaranteed to promote conflict. Many of our policies based on these hypotheses did promote conflict.

Let us first try to obtain a perspective on the state of knowledge in the 1980s. You are familiar with the exponential rate of population increase. It was an increase on a geometrical progression: the increase was a compound interest one. This same exponential rate of increase seemed to apply to the consumption of energy, to technical developments, to communication growth and to many areas in which largely empirical knowledge was applied. Perhaps the same exponential rate applied, also, to phenomena that related to population and technological increases, the movement to cities and industrialization. If it applied to these, it is likely because of the causal connections, to have applied, also, to levels of violence, the erosion of authority and many other social and political conditions that characterized developed politico-economic systems and led to the condition you now experience.

This exponential growth in population was accompanied by a similar increase of research findings, articles, books and theses on aspects of problems experienced in societies and the international system. The rate of increase in empirical knowledge, calculated by written work produced, was on this same exponential scale.

The great bulk of this outpouring frequently relied on the collection of and reference to highly specialized and descriptive empirical data. Foreign policy studies, historical studies, comparative political studies, strategic studies, institutional studies, regional studies, were within this empirical set.

Thus we appeared to have an explosion of empirical knowledge about problems that were themselves increasing on an exponential scale; but this did not appear to be accompanied by a similar explosion of theory, explanation, predictive power and policy insights relating to the problem areas being described. There appeared to be no significant increase in conceptual knowledge and in abilities to answer the key questions in political theory. Teaching syllabuses and conceptual notions employed in policy making, notions such as national interest, balance of power, rights and obligations, sovereignty and legality, were still anchored in the classics—Marx being about the most recent of a long line of philosophers who guided our thinking. Our teaching syllabuses and conventional wisdom implied that there had been no twentieth-century thinking. Our political models, both free enterprise and centrally planned, were models of past centuries. It would seem that the problems we faced, especially problems arising out of demands for political participation at all social levels—from the family to the international system—were increasing on a compound interest scale while our ability to solve them, even to think about them, was largely static. Indeed, it was regressive in the sense that the models and concepts were those developed in past and irrelevant political, economic and social environments and conditions. The 'There is nothing new under the sun' attitude abounded in the political sciences.

Amassed empirical knowledge is, from time to time, subject to significant shifts of thought. The gap between knowledge and reality then narrows and a great deal of this amassed empirical knowledge becomes irrelevant. In this way we manage to some degree to cope with the exponential increase (for example, antibiotics made irrelevant a body of knowledge and experience in the treatment of many diseases). However, such shifts were not the experience of political science. No general theories seemed to appear, no dramatic breakthroughs seemed to occur throughout the whole history of classical thought.

Let us take the cluster of problems, crime, terrorism, class conflict, racial conflict, communal or minority conflict and war. Each was studied separately, each had several separate literatures based on particular disciplines. At the applied level each was dealt with within a separate department of government and by separate agencies, as you know. Each was analysed from different points of view according to some model or theory that focussed on some particular aspect. Gurr (1970) had a deprivation theory of rebellion, Davis (1979) an expectation theory, Johnson (1966) was prepared to regard such phenomena as part of a rational process of change. There were aggression theories, theories about economic structures and others. Schools of thought spawn even more specialized studies. Little wonder that there was an exponential growth—but there were no generally accepted synthesizing theories.

There was a great inductive–deductive debate; but this did not lead to any change from this traditional analysis and description. The advice to refute rather than to find confirmation did not touch on the main problem: it merely advised on how to conduct the analysis of a situation and to arrive at a theory that related to some aspect of a problem. The inductive–deductive debate did not seem to touch on the problem of synthesis, the problems associated with dealing with phenomena that occur at different social system levels, as does violence. Were crime, terrorism, class conflict, racial conflict, communal and minority conflict and war separate phenomena or were they overt symptoms of some common phenomenon or set of phenomena?

Clearly it is not possible to move from one social system level to another if the units of analysis are institutions or structures. Small groups, communities, nations are wholly different in organization and structure. A separate disciplinary approach is convenient: psychology, economics, sociology and international relations are divisions based largely on organizational size. The problem could be overcome by taking the individual as the independent variable and the unit of analysis.

Is a synthesis possible between the individual as the independent variable and as the unit of analysis? There seemed to be a representative body of scholars, including Moore, Burns, Scarman, Peretz, Kelman, Sites, Bodenheimer, Epstein and Enloe who in their various disciplines of law, politics, sociology, anthropology and psychology, were forced to hypothesize some universal ontological human needs that *will* be satisfied by fair means or foul. This literature, which in fact was an exploding one, did seem to suggest a shift in thinking was taking place—perhaps for the first time in political science.

However, a shift of this order cannot take place in the absence of an articulated theory (such as control theory) and in the absence, also, of an alternative methodology that enables movement from one social level to another without the employment merely of analogy. It is this latter problem that is our present concern.

Let me explain by being anecdotal. I will trace out my own experiences and the experiences of my colleagues in the Centre for the Analysis of Conflict. I would claim that in so far as we made any contribution to behavioural studies it was that we tried to keep in touch with a wide literature. This experience was, therefore, a reflection of that literature and so it is only in presentation that this explanation of the methodological problem is to some degree anecdotal.

My discipline was international relations. This is a subject that was in disarray. At the beginning of the fifteen-year period I will review, it was highly inductive and lacking any significant theoretical framework. Teaching related mainly to diplomatic history, strategy, institutions, economic aspects of international relations, case studies and descriptions of decision making. The great 'traditional' versus 'behavioural' debates of the time were provoked by an emerging appreciation of the a-disciplinary nature of behavioural thought, by a questioning of descriptive and inductive processes of investigation and by a deviance that flouted the sanctity of the law as the reference point in any analysis of behaviour. Between the late 1960s and the 1980s some fundamental changes in thought took place; these were both epistemological and substantive and, in my view, justify the label 'paradigm shift'.

At a meeting in 1965 of British teachers of international relations, many or most of whom at that stage were historians, the 'traditionalists' challenged the 'behaviouralists' to offer an alternative approach by taking the Cuban missile crisis (which many of you will remember) and showing if there could be an improved analysis. This challenge was refused on the grounds that work based on the press and the documented 'records', compiled by those who were selecting and interpreting within a traditional framework, would not produce any different result. The challenge missed the whole point of the argument! Selection and interpretation of events is influenced by theoretical pre-dispositions. However, an undertaking was given to choose a situation and to examine it directly as it unfolded and on this basis to produce a report.

The situation chosen was the 'confrontation' between Indonesia, Malaysia and Singapore that was then current. Having cleared the position with the Prime Minister of the day, Harold Wilson, who had been endeavouring to promote some discussions, we invited the three governments concerned each to send three persons who would sit around the table with several of us so that we could look closely to the situation with a view to understanding more clearly the nature of inter-State relations. They responded and discussions took place over ten days with subsequent exchanges.

This was a case study. It was characterized by many of the features of traditional studies which we were criticizing. We had no theoretical framework. It was not surprising, therefore, that we derived very little from the exercise apart from having many of our previously held views confirmed. We should have anticipated that we had placed ourselves in this same traditional trap.

However, there was a productive accidental outcome. We were interested in observing a relationship at close quarters, not relying on the reports of others. Those who came to help us, however, appeared to have quite different motivations. They perceived the exercise as an informal, exploratory means of understanding their own conflictual problem and of trying to resolve it. Toward the end of the discussions we found ourselves in a third-party role for which we had not been prepared and for which we were ill equipped.

In 1966, therefore, we decided to examine another conflict situation and this time to prepare ourselves to enact the role of a third party within a problem solving framework. It was not to be a traditional bargaining and negotiation or mediation. It was to be a deep analysis of the relationships, made by the parties themselves, with our help as a third party. For these purposes we had to be prepared to inject information about behavioural relationships generally into the discourse and to draw attention to issues that could be missed. It was necessary, therefore, to gather together the seemingly relevant islands of theory and propositions that could be tested in this discourse and, at the same time, to be clear on the processes that would be followed in order to maintain this non-bargaining and analytical discussion.

At the time fighting in Cyprus was at a high level and the United Nations had not been able to bring the parties together. Mediation had consisted of going from one room to another with proposals and revised proposals. We cleared our intentions with the United Nations Secretariat and invited the (Greek Cypriot) President and the (Turkish Cypriot) Vice-President of Cyprus each to nominate three people who would sit around the table with us for these purposes. They came without delay and discussions went on for about a week. We had to give consideration to a variety of subjects: the various existing islands of theory; whether conflict was zero-sum when there were subjective factors of perception and interpretation and when there were hierarchies of values that were subject to change with additional information; the consequences of the two audience problem that leaders face when they make public statements; whether the values at stake were material or non-material, whether tactics or goals; what were the parties at different system levels and what were the issues relevant at each; to what extent was inter-State conflict a spill-over of domestic conflict; why had traditional mediation failed and so on. We believed we learned a lot. However, there was still no adequate theoretical framework, we had questions rather than answers. Nevertheless, we had guides to other areas of behavioural studies that would seem to be relevant.

By 1967 it was an opportune time to pull back from empirical work of this kind and to examine the main issues. In particular it was important to find out the extent to which both theory and process, which seemed to be relevant at these inter-State and inter-communal levels, were relevant to others—whether we were relying only on analogy or on some universal phenomena. It was possible to work with a team of industrial consultants, with London schools where teachers were being thrown down stairs, with police in their handling of first offenders, with the Northern Ireland Community Relations Commission and the various para-militaries. We were at this stage interested (in addition to the problem of levels of analysis) in the degree to which the values and needs that were being revealed in these different empirical studies were general and in the patterns of behaviour that seemed to re-emerge in each situation.

We were still without any theoretical framework that seemed adequate. We had no more than a selection of harmonious, yet unco-ordinated, islands of theory. In 1971 Steven Box of the University of Kent published his book on deviance. It seemed so relevant to studies of inter-State relations that we invited him to London to talk to our students. He did not, and probably still does not, know why he was invited and what was the connection between deviance and international relations. His work provided us with the framework for which we had been searching: a theory that incorporated power theory, one that placed conforming and non-conforming behaviour within the same framework, one that enabled us to adopt a no-fault and analytical approach to parties in a dispute, one that could explain the common patterns of behaviour that we had discovered, one that directed attention to the values and goals that parties appeared to have in common. A few years later, in 1973, Paul Sites articulated control theory as a general theory, not confined to deviance. As we have seen, he incorporated developmental theory and power theory in his exposition of needs theory and bond theory already implicit in Box. These contributions helped us to re-examine threat, coercion and deterrence theory and to realize that the power-deterrence framework of traditional international relations studies was based on false assumptions about human behaviour and dangerously midleading, consequently, in its applications.

It was clear that two such major contributions could not come out of thin air. The next task was to make a search of the literature in other areas. Here it was soon found that the same trends were apparent in anthropology, sociology, politics, law and, indeed, biology. They were also present in studies that could not be fitted into particular disciplines, such as those on rebellion and leadership and those on a variety of concepts such as justice, legitimacy, identity and nationalism.

What became clear from the inter-disciplinary literature was that many fundamental and consensually held assumptions were being challenged (for example, that societies are integrated wholes, that deterrence deters and, most important of all, that structure is the appropriate unit of explanation of political and social behaviour). The emergence of well-developed independence movements in Asia once Japanese occupation took place, and the sweeping away of colonialism in the post-World War II period could not be explained at the time other than by some myths about the far-reaching influence of Moscow. Within a control theory framework these developments were explicable. So, too, the way in which feudalism and other forms of domination had given place to systems in which human needs had found more expression, became explicable by reference to this needs-bonding theory that asserts that certain needs will be pursued, regardless of consequences to self and society, subject only to constraints imposed by valued relationships. The individual and his drives, not structure, seemed to be the unit of explanation.

The literature was signalling that we were at a stage of a significant shift in thinking. The implications of a shift from structure to the individual as the unit of explanation are far reaching. One could argue that this shift was not as sudden as this account would indicate, that the individual had always been a centre of attention. However, this, at least in my view, is a misreading of the history of thought. The individual involved in this shift was not the individual of classical thought that accepted the right of some to govern and others the obligation to obey, or the other individuals which, we have seen, were invented by economists, lawyers, psychologists and others to fit in with their theories. This individual who was becoming the unit of explanation, was the individual that revealed himself, his values and needs, by conforming, by being deviant, by being altruistic, by being violent, in short by behaving at all social levels, in all circumstances, in all times and doing all this as an integrated or a-disciplinary whole.

The inter-disciplinary literature was suggesting that the scientific quest was for laws of behaviour that were specific to the individual, not probabilities of behaviour. This would make possible what social and political science had been struggling for over the centuries and especially since the beginning of this scientific twentieth century, a non-ideological based, non-culturally based, non-normatively based explanation of behaviour.

Obviously, developmental theory would be the basis of a general theory that rested on human needs and their pursuit. Probably the hypothesis that was relevant was the self-evident one, and is exemplified by the cover of a book on child development, which showed a child a few months old exercising control over its mother by its movements (Stern, 1977). To adapt Sites' title 'Control [is] the basis of social order'. Given the hypothesis of control, a man from Mars, who knew nothing more of Earth than that there were living organisms who had the capacity to exercise control over others in the pursuit of survival and growth needs and who were constrained only by values attached to relationships that were a necessary consequence of this same survival goal, could deduce a general theory of behaviour that would apply at all social levels, including relations between Earth and Mars. In other words a general theory could be deduced from a self-evident hypothesis and without further empirical evidence.

However, such a view raised important methodological issues. From the beginning of the twentieth century there had been an attempt to be scientific in relation to politics, along with the belief that ultimately politics was subjectively based. A fundamental difference between natural and behavioural social sciences was widely accepted. At the same time there was an attempt to give an appearance of science by an emphasis on scientific method, that is the gathering of data, their analysis and the use of statistical devices to determine cause and effect. There had been a strong trend toward analysis and increased specialization, separate disciplines being a symptom of the latter. However, now we were moving toward a synthesizing hypothesis that was of a most axiomatic character as a means of explaining complex behaviour at all social levels. We were relegating scientific method and probability theory to a minor role in favour of hypothesizing a law, a natural law, concerning drives to survive, the drive to pursue certain human needs. The problem of analogy and the inductive–deductive controversy about testing and falsifying were being pushed aside in favour of a direct leap from a hypothesis to the deducation of a theory. How could we justify this?

The important Kuhn–Popper debate had seemed to contribute nothing to the methodological problems being experienced. This argument had focused to a large degree on the difference between verification and falsification. The reason why this particular issue attracted attention in the political sciences is understandable. Political theory and social sciences had generally been based on hypotheses that were arrived at within a cultural and structural framework that gave little attention to behavioural responses. There is such a thing as naive hypothesis forming no less than there is naive empiricism. Political science was dominated by hypotheses that hid assumptions and ignored obvious realities. Explanations of social integration in terms of coercion and share values had the hidden assumption that societies were integrated. Deterrence and social order theories hid the assumption that coercion and threat deter. Power theories assumed power balances were responsible for what peace existed and that relative power determined the behaviour of units within a system, despite overwhelming evidence and theoretical reasons which would lead one to suppose that there were values attached to cultural, traditional and other relationships entering into decision making. In these circumstances it was a reasonable reaction for philosophers like Popper and others to argue that a hypothesis is a personal matter of no scientific interest, that testing of a proposition was the focus of scientific interest.

This was, in practice, a despairing and even irresponsible response. It might not be of scientific interest that post-World War II political scientists adopted an ill-considered coercion hypothesis; but it was of practical significance if such an aggression–power hypothesis led to policies that were self-fulfilling. It was, also, a false response from a methodological point of view. The emphasis on testing was an irrelevance to subject matters in which there could be no testing by either verification or falsification. How could one have tested whether NATO deterred? Moreover, as Popper admitted, the personal nature of a hypothesis could not account for the progress science does make. Out of the infinite number of personal hypotheses that could be tested, somehow it happens that many fruitful ones are chosen.

If one were to reverse the Popper assertion and argue that it is the hypothesis that is the centre of scientific concern and that testing by 'scientific method' is of less importance, one would immediately be involved in consideration of the logical and scientific means of arriving at an hypothesis that would produce a rich, explanatory theory. One would clearly take care to arrive at a hypothesis that was fundamental in the sense that it related to behaviour in some fundamental aspect, an hypothesis that was self-evident in terms of our existing knowledge, an hypothesis that could be employed to deduce explanations of behaviour in increasingly complex situations, an hypothesis that was not hiding assumptions or cultural and consensual beliefs. The Box–Sites hypothesis and the theories they deduced seemed to be of this kind. Sites, in particular, had hypothesized certain basic human needs, all of which were deduced from some of the simplest and most obvious propositions about growth. Neither Box nor Sites was much concerned with testing in the conventional sense. Both lacked empirical data. Their strength was in their hypothesis and deductions from it. They could make direct jumps to prescription without the felt need for empirical evidence.

This was, in fact, what we had been doing while dealing with conflict situations such as Cyprus. Even the islands of theory on which we had relied for so long had virtually no empirical basis. The answer to the question 'How do you know?' had always to be in terms that appeared to be only analogy. We were, in effect, seeking some explanation of hypothesis formation, a science of hypothesis making.

Unknown to us at the time—we are ashamed to admit—were the works of Peirce and his notion of abduction or retroduction. Peirce, the son of a Harvard mathematician in the second half of the last century, a first class honours graduate in philosophy who could not get an academic job because he did not dress and behave according to the norms, published only a few articles during his life of editing. On his death he left a completed work and very many articles which are now widely available. They have been the subject of over 100 books and every year there is an increased interest in them. While he entertained several somewhat mystical explanations of how hypotheses that are rewarding come to be selected, his abductive approach was, in practice, what scholars in many different fields had, by the late 1950s and 1960s, been forced or led to adopt. He had articulated the approach by logical reasoning, whereas they had come to it by experience. His emphasis on hypothesis formation as a scientific enterprise served to explain and to justify what would in other circumstances be perceived to be outside the traditionally accepted methodological framework.

It will be clear that over fifteen years we had reversed the logical order of thought, step by step being forced back and back from empiricism and so-called scientific method to hypothesis forming and a process of deduction that enabled new material to be incorporated in a logical syllogism. All of our efforts had, in effect, been hypothesis formation. This experience seems to support Peirce's contention that a useful hypothesis is the result of, and not just the beginning of, a scientific process.

It seems to me that by the 1980s we were at the stage at which the steps I have traced out, which were our experience but which were consistent with academic experiences generally during this period, could be retraced in the other direction. We could now be scientific and logical. To do this we would have to take abduction on board as part of our methodology, arrive at a hypothesis that we knew in advance would produce rich results by reason of the work that had been done in arriving at it, deduce a general theory from it, such as the control theorists had made available, and move to process, to application without undue concern for the ordinary and usually inapplicable procedures of testing. Testing is in application prediction and processes involved in application, for it is these that make further theoretical refinements possible.

It will be immediately clear that Sites and others had hypothesized human needs just as natural scientists once hypothesized the particles of the atom. It was still not possible to give operational definitions and demonstrate their existence. As with atomic theory, the usefulness of behavioural theories—such as control theory—is in their richness in explanation and prediction.

The application of a needs-bond theory, as we have seen, centres around inter-active decision making (that is, processes that involve all parties affected before decisions are made). This is the process that encapsulates the set of human needs —stimulus, recognition, identity and security. These are the problem solving processes that we, by accident, applied when we had parties to disputes analysing their relationships. They are the processes that were being introduced into industrial relations and into community relations. Along with them was an interest in smallness of organizations despite economies of scale and opportunities for specialization. These processes had implications for the future of minority-majority relationships within so-called democratic majority government political systems, such as Northern Ireland. Such processes had implications that touch upon the notion of legitimacy, of justice, of freedom, of national interest and gave each a new meaning and the possibilities of operational definitions. There were within this needs framework, means of assessing both the possibilities of achieving goals and the means towards goals, leaving it to value-oriented politicians to decide whether they were prepared to impose on communities the consequences of pursuing unobtainable goals and costly means. A basis was provided for the analysis of revolt, rebellion and revolution in addition to deviant behaviour, however defined. There was, within this framework, an indication of the kind of 'Second Track' required to accompany the single-track power relationships of major States so that arms problems and conflicts within spheres of interest could be resolved outside power confrontations. We will return to the 'Second Track' idea.

It is my view that what was being achieved in these various methodological and substantive areas gave reason for believing that we were at long last beginning to move towards a non-ideological, non-normative, value free social science. Too late I fear, but of great interest and concern to you.

PART II: WAR AVOIDANCE POLICIES

System Imperatives

Decision makers usually consider that they are in control—subject only to certain obvious pressure groups and interests. Decision making theory assumes this to be the case. The reactive and inter-active models we have already considered imply rational decision making by decision makers. In practice, there are institutional processes that operate which limit choices progressively: choice becomes more and more limited as situations develop. Take, for example, the decision by the Japanese Cabinet to attack Pearl Harbour. This same Cabinet had been most restrained in the face of competitive currency devaluations and tariff wars. Individually, its members were opposed to siding with the Axis Powers and to acting against the West. As a decision-making group, however, they had no option. Cut off from raw material and markets, Japan could not avoid the most disastrous falls in living standards, which were not high anyway. They had nothing to lose and possibly something to gain by joining the Axis Powers and by trying to capture valuable sources of raw material and markets. Their decision was a direct result of decisions taken by Britain and other colonial powers to reserve their colonial markets for their industries in the Great Depression of the 1930s.

Or take the Great Depression that itself led to these events. Given the party political system, given the economic conditions that emerged largely as a result of World War I, given the private enterprise system and the limited abilities of Western Governments to plan their way out of unemployment, the policy of protection of colonial markets and the home market was inevitable.

Given the invention of nuclear weapons, there are logical developments, which lead to more and more escalation, then to deterrent strategies in which each Power struggles for a balance in its favour, then to winning strategies, and then to any actions necessary, including pre-emptive strikes, that ensure winning. The options become more limited as the course of events unfolds. Attempts to turn back by arms control, disarmament or political initiatives cannot alter the step-by-step logically justifiable escalation of war preparation. By the end of the 1970s many of us were predicting war. Many of you must have realized that you were on a train you could not stop and with few, if any, track changes available. The examples given above indicate that institutional processes have a continuity: World War I led to decisions that led to depression that led to war—there is no starting point or 'cause'.

There are many such continuing trends and courses. Innovation and invention give rise to industry; this brings workers together and cities are created, services are in demand and cities become bigger; this gives rise to alienation and crime. Size alone is sufficient to create social problems, regardless of social policies. All of these trends and processes taken together and left to themselves to operate without offsetting planning, lead to disaster for civilizations, as recent experiences would seem to suggest. It was such trends and processes that led to the extinction of many past species. The process that once led to a meteorite colliding with Earth and destroying much of life was of the same order. It could happen again in the absence of planned interception.

We have already argued that there are specific human drives that *will* be satisfied. These have given rise to trends that are also inexorable, from slavery to serfdom, to we–they relations in industry, to socialism and, if civilizations survive, to social structures in which such human drives or needs will be satisfied.

We have, therefore, many kinds of short-term trends (short in an evolutionary perspective) that give rise to social problems and serious conflicts. We have, also, long-term trends toward the fulfilment of certain human needs that make possible the harmonious behaviour of individual groups within a system. All these trends and processes taken together would seem to lead to disaster in the short and medium terms, though leading to the appropriate social structures in the long term because of drives that *will* be satisfied. Our problem, therefore, is to find means of dealing with the short- and medium-term problems in ways that enable the long-term trends to take control.

This perspective helps in defining the problems we face. Our concern is with problems of change, the challenges that are made to institutions and structures by the continuing pressure of behavioural drives that are continuously operating. This would not be difficult if there could be an accurate costing of the consequences of the frustration of human needs. If the consequences of resistance to change were clearly perceived, then adjustments would be made such as to reduce costs to all concerned. Rarely is this the case. The problems of costing in the absence of an adequate theory of behaviour are very great. Take industrial disputes: if the end result were known in advance it would be possible to arrive at a settlement without the intervening costs of the dispute.

In addition to the lack of foresight due to the absence of knowledge of behaviour, there is a time element. In pre-World War III times there was resistance to independence movements. This led to violent struggles for 'liberation'. There were North–South conflicts over resource development and distribution, there were Middle East and South African conflicts over identity and recognition claims. Each generation of elites considered they could 'win'. In any event from their point of view, the costs were costs to another generation: winning was a short-term gain to existing elites. The problem civilizations face, therefore, is the problem of finding adequate theories on which to predict behaviour and the outcome of conflict. This requires processes by which parties can make reliable estimates of costs by means of inter-action that give them reliable information about the motives and perceptions of other parties.

However, the realities are that elites are resistant to change even where there are theories that explain and from which it is possible to predict, even when, indeed, there are problem-solving processes that enable them to perceive, and to define accurately. There are 'ideological' commitments and role positions to maintain. The Western–Soviet relationship was characterized by such resistances. In retrospect, what was the conflict about? As Boulding pointed out in the 1960s, the dialectic exchange was unscientific and irrelevant. There were certain features in each system that were relevant to human needs; it was not an either–or choice. Yet both sides seemed to make it so. Even as an either–or choice, what was the conflict about? Both systems were changing rapidly under pressure of human needs that were demanding satisfaction. There were resistances, it is true, but the trends were clear even in the life of one person. Both sides, nevertheless, felt obligated to defend their systems against all modifications in case this allowed the other to 'win'. This led to a crude form of power politics and thermonuclear strategies with their inevitable and logical result.

Consequently, we are led to this deterministic explanation based on inexorable trends that are destructive in the shorter term despite the potential in the long term. We must accept this degree of determinism: to argue otherwise, as many were doing on an ideological basis in the pre-World War III period, is being quite unreal. So unreal and irrelevant was the well-meaning opposition to power policies that they were of little or no influence: there was no progress made on arms control, there was no improvement in great Power relationships. We are dealing with trends that have no origin, institutional trends that cannot be diverted into other tracks, conditions that cannot be affected by changed governments or structures, trends that have a continuity and a logic inherent within them.

Let us go back to the example of the situation leading to a meteorite striking Earth. There is nothing that can be done about the problem: it will persist and always present the probability of the destruction of the Earth. However, it is possible to do something about the danger, not by altering the situation itself, but by creating a new one by which such a meteorite is intercepted some days before collision. So it is with systems of behavioural processes. The answer to the apparent determinism and fatalism of processes which cannot be stopped or diverted, is the creation of other competing processes, which have the potential to stop and to divert existing ones. In the pre-World War III situation it was as unreasonable to advocate the stopping of arms production as it was to stand in the way of an on-coming vehicle in order to stop it. However, it is possible to create and bring alongside another vehicle and from this vantage point to exercise some control.

In practice we do this on a small scale quite frequently.

When we can accurately perceive the results of behaviour we find means to modify behaviour. When children are being destructive or are acting in ways dangerous to them, they are diverted by competing distractions. The positive handling of deviant behaviour is to provide other activities that give some sense of fulfilment. Grazing grasses are controlled by introducing competitive species. Breeding to a desired form is done by introducing new strains. There should be some conceptual term for this tactic because it is so general. We do not seem to have one that expresses the mutative influence of alternative systems. For convenience I propose to call this the 'Second Track' and this is the subject of the next section.

The Second Track

So far in this epistle we have not made much progress with war avoidance—which is the final object of high-level policy. However, we have a theoretical framework and its philosophical support. Now let us look to this core problem.

It was always widely accepted in Western political thought that violence, including warfare, was, in the last resort, a legitimate means either of bringing about change or of preserving existing orders. Power balances and deterrence strategies were always pursued to decrease the incidence of violence of war; but they were never relied upon to prevent it.

By the 1980s, the costs of deterrent strategies and the likely consequence of major war were such that this view could no longer sensibly be accepted as unchallengeable. 'Sensibly' is judgemental. This power politics view was undoubtedly 'rational'. Indeed, it was widely accepted even in the thermonuclear age. Calculations were made of percentage of populations likely to survive, plans were made—in which you took part—to protect decision makers and control centres. Some of those who could afford them built personal shelters. In this rational sense thermonuclear war is no different in kind from other forms of war. The difference is merely in levels of destruction. Perhaps it was never 'sensible' to accept the classical view that war was a legitimate extension of diplomacy and power politics. Perhaps it was only this greatly increased level of destruction that forced us to consider options that should have been considered even in the days of bows and arrows.

This classical and traditional view that war is a legitimate instrument of last resort stemmed from the belief that relations between nations were determined, finally, by the balance nations make between their interests and the relative power, economic and military, at their disposal. A small Power had limited means to pursue its interests, a Great Power had a dominating position. Two Great Powers, each with an 'overkill' capacity, presented an unprecedented relationship. In theory there should have been assured deterrence. In practice, as we now know, if the authorities in one feel so threatened either internally or externally that they have nothing to lose by the gamble of war, then deterrence does not deter.

There was, consequently, a crisis in thought and in policy. A seemingly universal and rational philosophy and the policies based on it, appeared to be dysfunctional and not 'sensible'. Holocaust occurred—after it was accepted that 'deterrence' does not deter or after you ceased to talk about deterrence in 1981 and talked about 'winning'. What strategic policies will you follow?

Clearly no Great Power will be diverted from its deterrence strategies. Disarmament and arms control measures cannot be effective at least until there is no longer a felt need for arms. At the same time, negotiations between major Powers, such as the Strategic Arms Limitation Talks (SALT), led to escalation of tensions and of arms levels because of the nature of bargaining within a power politics framework.

Let us go back to what we were beginning to believe before World War III. In 1981 we thought some middle and smaller nations could disarm unilaterally and adopt a neutral stance in the then current United States–Soviet Union power struggle. One consequence could have been to shift the political and strategic balance and to alter the strategic planning of major Powers. In order to pursue their power strategies both of these major forces would have, therefore, to offer something more than power strategies that involve smaller nations as platforms and targets.

In these circumstances there was thought to be a felt need by major Powers for a 'Second Track', that is a means both of reducing the risks by war between them and of creating an improved image among their client nations.

A Second Track, in our view then, consisted of a set of related activities:

(i) A continuing means of communication between the main protagonists at an unofficial level so that there can be exploratory discussions in private, without commitment, on all matters that give rise to tensions between the major Powers—internal conditions, problems occurring in developing States, energy problems, SALT and others.
(ii) A continuing dialogue on the internal problems faced by major Powers.
(iii) A 'Blue Cross', a semi- or non-official organization, which like the Red Cross in relation to disaster situations, can offer a problem solving service in relation to conflicts within and between nations.
(iv) A training centre for people undertaking such work.
(v) A research establishment that provides the back-up for problem solving techniques in all these three areas.

This Second Track was in no sense an alternative to the first. Power politics strategies would be pursued. The Second Track was to run in parallel, hopefully becoming more and more significant and finally becoming the dominant track in due course, supplanting the conventional policy of the time.

DEAR SURVIVORS

The idea of a Second Track attracted me when in Moscow just after the 1980 intervention by the Soviet Union in Afghanistan. It became clear after discussions with officials and non-officials that what was intended as a constructive intervention, designed to improve relations between the Government and the Islamic people of that country, went wrong. It went wrong, as such attempts so frequently do, for unanticipated reasons, in this case a totally unexpected event—the assassination of the then Prime Minister in circumstances that pointed to his former supporters (who had felt betrayed by him) as being the culprits. The actual details are unimportant now. What concerned me was:

(i) that there had been no communication about such an important intervention to other States, especially to the United States, which would be deeply concerned and;
(ii) that there had been no communication when unexpected circumstances destroyed the legitimacy of the enterprise. There was a 'hot line' but it was not used. Nor was there any informal communication to embassies which remained, not merely in the dark, but speculating and presumably reporting in ways that merely reflected their various stereo-typical attitudes.

Apparently, it was not possible for governments to admit to mistakes and failures or to communicate intentions, even when they believed that they were acting with the highest motives. In this sense diplomacy was not a useful institution. Diplomacy at close quarters was a most inept means of information gathering and communication, especially where there were more or less closed systems, as was the case with the Soviet Union. Speculation, guesses over dinners and at parties, become 'informed' opinion and knowledge from 'reliable sources'. With the type of communication between governments that the technological age made possible, formal diplomacy was out-moded and probably dysfunctional.

THE LETTER

Communication at all official levels was frequently distorted, especially in conditions in which bargaining positions were being adopted. The Test Ban Treaty commenced as a confrontation between the United States, who maintained that inspection was required to differentiate between underground tests and natural earth movements and the Soviet Union who argued that it was unnecessary. When scientists from both sides met in Moscow in 1962, those from the United States adopted the official American viewpoint while those from the Soviet Academy of Sciences adopted the Soviet argument. So strong was the bargaining or negotiating tradition that it took days before even these scientists could remove themselves from the political environment. When they did there was agreement.

The whole area of inter-State communication should be re-examined. The first track of power politics and diplomatic bargaining and negotiating will continue; but it needs to be supplemented by far more intense exchanges between those who are specialists in their fields and not the diplomatic 'generalists'. (You may recall that the Duncan Report published by the British Government in 1969 argued that 'with certain important exceptions—e.g., The Legal Advisers—we do not believe that the Diplomatic Service should be made up of experts. Its members should remain generalists.')

There are some practical advantages in unofficial exchanges. Scholars are expendable, their activities can be brushed aside if not productive, they can be made use of if productive. As scholars they have their own reputations at stake: they can be counted on to argue their case within a framework which they are prepared to defend. They can be analytical in ways that would seem irrelevant to officials, they can question assumptions and explore options without commitment. This is a resource that was not exploited enough, though there was at least sufficient experience to justify greater exploitation.

DEAR SURVIVORS

In his speech in 1981, the President of the Soviet Union called for closer communication between scientists from both sides:

> The peoples must know the truth about the destructive consequences for humankind of a nuclear war. We suggest that a competent international committee should be set up, which would demonstrate the vital necessity of preventing a nuclear catastrophe. The committee could be composed of the most eminent scientists of different countries. The whole world should be informed of the conclusions they draw.

It is reasonable to argue that a body of scholars, who in the normal course have means of communication with relevant authorities on an informal basis, could help in analysing the complexities of relationships as a whole and in communicating details of particular crisis situations as they emerge.

There were several attempts to establish regular meetings at informal levels. Indeed, my colleagues at the Centre for the Analysis of Conflict, with the support of the British Council, pursued a programme of exchanges over several years. There was never a continuing seminar comprising scholars from both the United States and the Soviet Union. Ideally, it should be possible for selected scholars each to remain for (say) one month. This would result in regular replacements selected in the light of events, sometimes a strategist, sometimes a Third World specialist, sometimes an economist, sometimes a specialist on a current crisis situation. For special purposes scholars could stay longer, others could be invited, for example, members of embassies and administrations and scholars from other countries.

Detailed reports on discussions could be made available to participants, past and present, so that newcomers would be fully briefed and others would be kept informed. Appropriate reports could also be made available to relevant practitioners. In this way continuity would be maintained and an extending community generated. A secretariat could make regular summaries of new books and articles on subjects of relevance and these, also, could be made available to participants and practitioners.

The Second Track has a domestic component. This letter has concentrated on international issues, because we are concerned primarily with war avoidance. However, it would be a mistake to think that war avoidance was solely or even primarily an international matter. Imagine, if there had been no internal dissent in the Soviet Union due to their failure to solve the participatory problem and if there had been no internal employment and income distribution problems in the capitalist countries, would war have occurred? I think not. World War II was preceded by unemployment and a host of internal problems that had their spill-over effect. Hitler was the creation of an unemployment problem. We have previously observed that there are institutional processes that are continuing—they cannot readily be interrupted. Parts of these processes that lead to international conflict compromise these internal problems. A Second Track, therefore, has to be concerned with domestic problems no less than with international ones.

It may seem far-fetched to you to imagine capitalist and socialist co-operation in helping to solve the internal problems each experiences. However, this is probably the essence of war avoidance. In a power politics interaction the tendency is to take advantage of internal weaknesses. We had no difficulty in agreeing in principle that there should be co-operation in the reduction of arms and in solving problems in spheres of interest. What we did not seem to realize is that the solution of internal problems is in the mutual interest of conflicting parties in a world of thermonuclear capacities. Experience shows that international action is a defence against internal collapse. A function of the Second Track is to prevent this happening, to create internal security as a means toward international co-operation. Societies are never so different that each has not something to learn from the other. Scholars of different States are not so remote from the fundamental problems of making the best use of scarce resources in any set of structural circumstances that they could not be helpful one to the other.

The Role of Middle Powers

It is not difficult to visualize the post-World War III international system. Despite these warnings and advices there will be a continuing trend in the pre-holocaust power politics. There will be the dominant power rivalry track at least until the operations of the Second Track start to take control. So this section is written on the assumption that the world system will evolve in much the same way as it did before its third major catastrophe.

It is almost certain that a Second Track is politically and technically impossible in the absence of some third-party initiative and a continuing third-party mediating role. It seems likely, also, that there cannot be any solution to the thermonuclear problem and the avoidance of war unless thermonuclear Powers are denied the bases and targets that are made available to them by reason of alliance structures. For these reasons you should consider whether 'middle Powers' could make a positive contribution to peaceful relations between major Powers by moving toward strategic and foreign policies of independence.

There are negative reasons for a policy of independence and unilateral actions, in particular to avoid being used by other Powers in their power struggles and to keep out of their conflicts. There are also positive reasons. Sweden used to argue that its neutralism was a positive one in the sense that it was in a position to suggest and to assist politically and to contribute to peace keeping. Switzerland's neutrality enabled an organization, the Red Cross, to operate with more credibility than would have been the case had it not been based on neutral soil. The non-aligned States argued initially that their status enabled them to make policy judgements freely, in favour of—or in opposition to—the policies of Great Powers, according to the merits of each case. It was, in their view, an 'active neutralism'.

Both the negative and positive aspects of the neutralism of each country reflect both the interests and the history of the foreign policies of the States concerned. Neutralism in international affairs was the policy of the Indian Congress Party many years before India was independent. The policies of Sweden, Finland, Austria, Switzerland developed out of their geographic positions and relationships with other States. The non-aligned States were predisposed in this direction on attaining independence. Neutrality and neutralism, where they existed, were extensions of policies of States, not something alien or out of character and merely an ideological commitment on the part of a temporary ruling party.

If 'middle Powers' were to be independent of alliances it would only be because this was a logical development of their policies in the context of world affairs. Each would adopt its own particular form of neutralism. Each would play its own distinctive role. Its independence would, inevitably, be a continuation of its past policies, reflecting past and present interests, relationships and values. It would not be a neutrality of the Austrian type, which was a defensive neutrality bordering on isolation, or the cautious neutrality of Finland. It would be an independence that reflected past relationships. It would be an approach to world affairs calculated to further these relationships in its own interests and in their interests. To the extent that it were a marked change in policy or a seeming discontinuity, it would be a change in tactics rather than purposes. It would be an approach calculated to strengthen relationships, including trading relationships, and to take advantage of experience in world affairs in the promotion of those conditions that appeared to be most in its interests.

If middle Powers were neutral for these reasons of interest, they would be obligated to go further than the positive neutralism of the non-aligned, further than merely being in a position to make judgements on the merits of cases. They would be obligated to intervene as a third party, to prevent and to help resolve disputes. As world Powers and as world trading nations, this would be the main interest and the main motivation for an independent position. As a great military Power, Britain, for example, had a power and a balancing role. As a less powerful State, yet one that still had widespread interests, its role could have been to remain one that contributed to law and order and peaceful relations by techniques that did not rest on military power.

If middle Powers were to be neutral for these purposes, various consequential issues would be raised. What precisely is this positive role of conflict resolution? To what extent would the need to be supportive of all parties to disputes and to take an objective view of each conflict be incompatible with traditional relationships, viewpoints and values? If an East–West division evolved again, to what extent would a positive third-party role be seen to be in the general Western interest, acceptable and supported? If so accepted, to what extent would it be suspect from an Eastern point of view? Is the role of the State to provide the necessary conditions for a private Red Cross type organization concerned with conflict resolution rather than to enact this role itself? What alterations in selection and training of Foreign Office personnel would be required? What would be the role at the United Nations or like body?

This approach and set of questions takes the debate out of the deterrents–unilateralist disarmament framework, which it was in during the 1980s. The issue is not whether a middle Power should, in its own interests, opt out of alliances and independent deterrents. It is whether it can make a more effective contribution to its own security and to the security of the international community by itself enacting a third party role or, alternatively, by providing the environment in which an appropriate non-official organization could enact such a role. The unilateralist position was negative, it ignored the perceived realities of capitalist–communist conflict. Even the less radical independent deterrent position was unacceptable for the same reasons. To argue that a middle Power could have its own deterrent, independent of the United States, was a difficult one to sustain in practice. In any event such a middle Power would not have been perceived as being independent in a crisis.

It is possible to bring the two approaches together: there could be an independent and armed middle Power with this positive role, provided the level and nature of defence forces were such as clearly to be defensive and not such as could tip the balance one way or another should there be conflict. Indeed, a sophisticated peace-keeping force could, if the parties were to agree, be a part of a third-party conflict resolving role.

Problem Solving

When discussing the Second Track we introduced the idea of problem solving approaches. The notion of problem solving ties together much of what has been argued in this letter. Problem solving—unlike bargaining and negotiation—is a process designed to enable parties to a dispute to differentiate tactics from goals, to separate wants from needs, to sort out objective and subjective differences in interest, to determine perceptions and misperceptions, to define zero-sum and potential positive-sum outcomes of conflict. The interactive models of decision making contained in the section dealing with control theory and industrial relations are meaningful only in the context of problem solving. Also, the role of the 'middle Powers' introduced in the last section rests on this notion of problem solving and the role of the third party in relation to it.

Problem solving approaches

I have argued that judicial settlement, arbitration, mediation and conciliation are conflict settlement processes that are generally unacceptable because they take decision making out of the hands of the parties concerned. What is the problem solving alternative?

This is a complex subject, not because the answer proves to be complex, but because of the traditions and assumptions that have to be brushed aside before the obvious answer is revealed. For example, we have assumed that conflict is zero-sum—that there must be winners and losers. Underlying this assumption has been another, that conflict arises over disputes about finite resources. This has been our conventional wisdom, and it is certainly how parties to a dispute viewed their conflicts. In practice the assumptions appear not to be justified.

In fact, conflicts involve many values and costs. Hierarchies of values alter according to circumstances and knowledge, making conflicts subjective in character. Pay-offs and trade-offs alter options. There are, also, problems of perception and interpretation of the behaviour and motivations of others, adding to the subjectivity of conflict. Furthermore, the true motives are usually ill-defined in that the means and the ends become mixed. A strategic piece of territory may be important for security; but security might be attainable by other means. A conflict could arise over it even though it would not be valued if the perceived threat were removed by resolving the underlying conflict. In most cases of social interaction (for example, industrial conflict), the gain of one side does not equal the loss of the other; there are behavioural variables that render interaction far more complicated than this. Solutions are possible that enable both sides to gain—as, for example, when conditions of industrial peace lead to increased productivity. Management was becoming aware of this and far more attention was being given to forms of participation by employees that previously would have been thought to amount to a loss of management, but which after experience was claimed to be a gain.

These trends away from treating conflict as zero-sum, were determining the trends within behavioural studies. If we were to draw two axes, the x axis representing coercion at the negative extreme and co-operation and participation of the subjects at the positive end and the y axis representing, at the negative extreme, solutions to conflicts where the gain of one side equals the loss of the other and at the positive end gains to both sides, then we would have four quadrants that depict approaches to social problems (see Figure 3). On the bottom left would be compulsory settlements of disputes where there were apparently irreconcilable conflicts of interests: this was how social problems were once regarded and tackled. On the top left would be conditions in which even conflicts that could be settled to the advantage of all parties had to be determined by an outside agent and enforced. On the bottom right would be conditions in which no solutions were possible because there were conditions of irreconcilable conflicts of interests

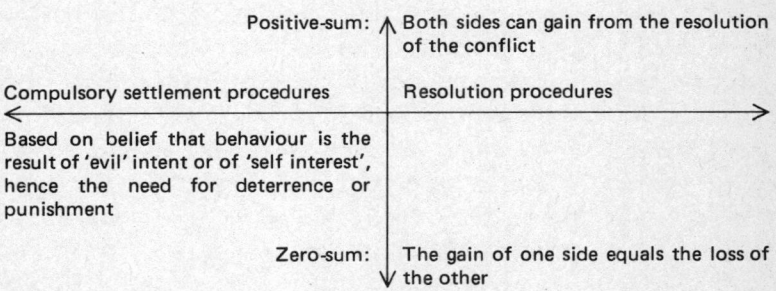

Figure 3 Approaches to social problems

and no authority to impose settlements. This is a condition of anarchy and we may describe international relations in these terms. On the top right there would be a condition in which conflicts had a solution that would satisfy all parties and which would, therefore, be maintained without enforcement.

It is in this last segment that problem solving approaches would fit. However, instead of it being assumed that States could solve problems peacefully, this face-to-face technique assumes that there are misperceptions of relationships and inadequate information about alternative means and alternative goals and that institutionalized means are required to enable States to reperceive and to obtain information about the motivations and goals of each other. The underlying assumption is that States are not in themselves a cause of conflict, or are aggressive or power motivated, but that they are responding to their environment within the limits of the knowledge they have available about their interests and the responses of others. Given perfect knowledge of responses of others or tested theories and rules of conduct that could act as a substitute for perfect foresight, States would avoid any conflicts that were more costly than alternative means of achieving their goals.

The traditional arbitrator or mediator made orders or proposals and believed that he/she was applying principles of justice and reasonableness. Whenever important interests were at stake the mediator failed to bring agreement between parties concerned. Courts made judgements which purported to apply principles; but only after argument and disagreement as to what the principles were and how they should be applied. There was no certainty and in any event the decisions were legal ones that did not necessarily reflect the motivations and interests of the people concerned, resulting in outcomes that were not regarded by them as just or appropriate. Policy makers endeavoured to decide what was just and politically feasible. This subjective approach had more to do with the interests of the decision makers than of the parties affected by the decisions. It is only the parties concerned that can make the judgements necessary as to how to interpret principles.

This is not to suggest that the mediator has no role or that the decision maker is not required to make decisions. On the contrary, the mediator and the decision maker have two particular, professional, exacting leadership roles to perform —far more exacting and responsible than those traditionally associated with mediation and decision making. These are, first, to articulate and to translate into terms that are relevant to a particular situation the pure theory—the principles on which decision making in behavioural relationships must take place (described here as need and relationship theory); secondly they have the role of ensuring that the parties concerned are involved and that their involvement is a problem-solving one and not one of confrontation, competition, bargaining or power.

This third-party or leadership behaviour involves decision making by injecting knowledge into the communication between parties; it is the application of problem solving techniques to decisions made by parties; it is the means by which the total involvement of all those subject to decisions becomes part of the decision making process.

Problem solving has several distinctive characteristics. First, the solution is not a final end product. It is itself another set of relationships that contains its own sets of problems. The problem of growth can be solved deliberately to give rise to problems of leisure that have then to be solved. A cybernetic process might achieve growth; but a set of unanticipated problems such as inequalities and class conflict might be the actual outcome. Second, problem solving frequently requires a new synthesis of knowledge, new techniques and a change in theoretical structure. When deviance cannot be contained by coercion, a quite different strategy based on a quite different analysis is called for. Third, the system of inter-actions is an open one (that is, the parts are subject not merely to interaction among themselves, as is the case with a metal puzzle, but to inter-action with a wider environment over which there can be no control). It is the open nature of behavioural systems that is part of the problem. Employer–employee relationships occur in a wider political, economic and social environment, are affected by them and affect them.

Because of this complexity there was always a tendency to 'solve' social and political problems by the more direct and simple reactive process (that is, by making adjustments as and when seems necessary, as the situation changes). It is also the reason why there was such a strong tendency to deal with social and political problems by the direct means of coercion.

The traditional approach in the social sciences is for the observer or analyst to stand outside the situation or events being studied. The observer sees the situation in terms of his own standards, his own interpretations of behaviour, his own knowledge of history, sociology, politics and so on. However, it is the common patterns of the behaviour of those involved which are the subject of study, not the common patterns of their apparent behaviour as seen by outsiders. The only reality that is relevant is that of the subjects. For example, only those involved in a conflict can judge which variables are relevant, which patterns of behaviour are applicable. The conflict to be resolved is that which is identified as the conflict by the parties involved. Their interpretations of behaviour and events are part of the reality. Clearly they are likely to alter their view and interpretations with increased knowledge. If the resolution of the problem can be assisted by a more informed dialogue between those involved or by injections of information by a third party, then the 'reality' will alter.

We are led, therefore, to seek processes in which observations of patterns of behaviour are made from within the situation, by the parties themselves. These same conditions are those in which knowledge about patterns of behaviour can be fed back to parties, allowing them to select what is perceived to be relevant and giving them the opportunity to alter their selection as new information seems to require.

These conditions suggest themselves. The parties need to be placed in conditions which enable them to check on their perceptions of each other and the social order they are confronting, to assess the costs of pursuit of their goals in terms of loss of other values and to explore alternatives that are available once this reperception and reassessment have taken place. The third party is an observer in a scientific role. He/she makes no assessment, judgements, suggestions or interventions except to communicate what may be relevant patterns of behaviour drawn from other situations. The third party is wholly supportive of all actors, and adopts a no-fault position. His/her knowledge of the situation is confined to the perceptions of the actors, conflict being a perceived relationship, even though it usually has structural components.

In short, the contribution of social science to problem-solving has been to detail a process for the analysis by the parties of their situation and to provide specific information, the relevance of which is to be determined by the parties. The answer to the question 'What is the solution to a particular behavioural problem and what should be done?' is 'There is a process to be followed, including the making available of all those pieces of knowledge which the actors find relevant and significant'. The particular and detailed outcome of this process is unknown in advance even to the parties. It is likely to be very different from their expectations because of likely changes in preferences and cost assessments. However, it is an outcome which emerges as a result of knowledge of the motivation of all concerned, the costs of pursuit of goals and whatever relevant knowledge about organizational behaviour that exists.

The role of the third party has little relationship to the

traditional notion of a mediator or judge. Rather than work from ascertained 'facts' or norms and practice in a particular situation, the attempt by the third party is to apply generalizations about conflict to the particular situation being examined, thereby helping to analyse it. Its role is confined to feeding in information about conflicts in general and is not concerned with suggesting 'solutions' or arriving at assessments. There is an implied assumption that the analysis of a particular conflict, within this analytical framework, itself leads to the resolution of the conflict. There is a hypothesis that once relationships have been analysed satisfactorily, once each side is accurately informed of the perceptions of the other, of the alternative values and goals, of the alternative means and costs of attaining them, the possible outcomes acceptable to the parties are revealed.

The third party or facilitator also has an initiating and structuring role. Tentative assessments must be made as to which are the parties and which are the issues relevant to these parties that are to be discussed. Typically deviant behaviour involves many parties in addition to those engaged in the deviant act. Juvenile crime involves parents, schools and peer groups, not just as parties that can assist the deviant in returning to conforming behaviour, but as causes of the deviance and as means by which the environment of the deviant can be altered. In this sense, authorities concerned with living and working conditions may be parties to the conflict involved. So, too, in wider conflicts. An industrial conflict involves many unions and many different levels of organization within unions, each of which experiences conflict within its organization and this applies to management too. It is the role of the facilitator to ascertain which parties are those that are most directly concerned, and to arrive at a tentative schedule of analysis that will ultimately take into account all parties and all issues. Traditional settlement tends to dwell on those parties that appear to be powerful, rather than on those directly concerned, as in the case of a communal dispute in which more powerful States are involved. Structuring communication between parties is an important role requiring some tentative analysis and perhaps some tentative judgements regarding the nature of the conflict and its probable origins (for further discussion see Burton, 1979; Mitchell, 1981).

The value issue

This analysis of the role of the third party raises an issue that affects those involved in industrial relations, social work, police administration and all others concerned with the management of conflict: is the objective of intervention to preserve systems and the interests of elites and authorities in them or to resolve conflict?

This value issue was raised by classical theory and the processes of mediation and settlement that flowed from it. There was an implied win–lose relationship in them, a special priority to be given to law and order and the observation of norms and, consequently, a tendency to preserve existing institutions, processes and relationships. Change could occur only when relative power made this possible. A problem solving approach, however, seeks outcomes that satisfy the informed aspirations and goals of all parties, without bargaining and compromise. These include change, for outcomes that conserve by reason of relative bargaining power can be self-defeating in the longer term. The value issue is not applicable to problem-solving. The values are the values of the parties in dispute as they emerge by acquiring knowledge of their relationships and possible outcomes. They are not the values of the third party. In a problem solving context the facilitator is supportive, non-judgemental and limited to interventions that make available insights which are deemed by the parties to be relevant or irrelevant.

It has been argued that processes of decision-making themselves influence or even determine outcomes. Reactive processes are an extension of traditional power politics theories. They are effective only when power is virtually absolute. This, as experience has shown, is not the case in politics or in industry. Associated with reactive processes are many assumptions that are not valid. Behavioural theory—control theory in particular—provides a more useful framework because it introduces considerations of political psychology and especially human needs that are to be satisfied if organizations are to be harmonious. Within this framework it is clear that perceived conflicts of interest are not necessarily zero-sum, for the goals sought are not mainly material ones. There are processes that assist in transforming apparently win-lose conflicts into ones that have positive outcomes, processes that enable re-definitions of situations as a result of conditions in which perceptions can be assessed, motivations of others ascertained, value hierarchies analytically costed and outcomes explored that are not considered within a power or bargaining framework. This is an analytical, problem-solving process. There is a special and professional role for a third party that is designed to ensure that parties operate within a problem-solving framework.

Conclusions are self-evident. A far greater amount of attention in training and management needs to be given to the complexities of problem solving and the relevant processes. By the 1980s there was a well-developed literature and a good deal of workshop experience, and there were also several specialist courses on problem solving available. A centre for the training of a new type of mediator, a professional qualification, will be required to cope with acute political situations, especially majority-minority situations, which finally lead to violence at a high level, regardless of the types of political decisions that might emerge in the post-War World III system. Problem-solving mediation, whether it be in the political area, the industrial or any other, is not reasonably the province of wholly untrained, unskilled, non-professional diplomats, politicians, industrialists and trade union officials, no matter what their charisma, status or personality. Societies, including subsystems like industries, will have to think in terms of professionally trained third parties that are valued by all sides of a conflict as a result of their professionalism and their knowledge of the rules of procedure and as a result of the outcomes that they make possible.

However, the requirement of every society that is likely to emerge in the future is wider. Problem solving techniques cannot develop and will not be acceptable in the absence of a wide understanding of them and a consensus about the nature of conflict and the relevance of problem solving. The reversion back to zero-sum notions and power bargaining tactics is always a real danger in the absence of a widespread knowledge of alternative notions and processes.

For this reason problem solving is a core ingredient of any forward-looking educational system. The political development of members of societies, and through them of societies, rests on their knowledge of problem solving. The three Rs—Reading, wRiting and aRithmetic—are inadequate without the fourth, Reasoning.

The 'Is' and the 'Ought'

The student of politics is always confronted with the problem of 'is' and 'ought' when endeavouring to be creative and prescriptive. In applied politics, if not philosophy, the 'ought' has to be avoided unless it is an extension of 'is'—otherwise it is unreal and impracticable. All that anyone can do is to advance the course of history, cut down on time lags, and in so doing perhaps help to avoid some of the accidents and mistakes that bring catastrophe.

The single track, the power politics approach, is an 'ought'. It is essentially normative, law and order 'ought' to be respected, nations 'ought' not to be aggressive, alliance members 'ought' to support their Great Power, human rights 'ought' to be observed—in short, the other side ought to behave according to the rules as interpreted by us. The world of the 'is' is a different world. It is the world in which certain human needs *will* be pursued, needs of security, identity, recognition, distributive justice, freedom. No legal or cultural norms can prevent this occurring—in the longer term. Yet the single power track has been the one with credibility: it was defined as 'political realism'.

The real political realism is that there 'is' a thermonuclear problem and there 'is' a logical inevitability of conflict if policies on both sides are confined to power politics strategies. There 'is' a felt need on both sides to control the consequences of these strategies by resolving conflicts within their spheres of interest, by resolving their own political and strategic conflicts. There 'is' a tested problem solving process by which this can be done. There 'is' a tendency, arising out of needs for identity and control, towards increased independence of middle Powers. Putting all this together does not make an 'ought': it will occur, unless in the meantime the delays that are likely without some deliberate initiatives give opportunities for accidents and mistakes that run counter in the short term to the trends that underlie relationships. There is a further 'is'. The kind of initiative required is not possible for a Great Power to take for fear of being thought, within a power bargaining framework, to be showing weakness. Middle and small Powers can enact this third-party role, with the help of professional facilitators. Scholars are expendable. They can afford to take initiatives, perhaps with the private connivance of governments, and they can afford to fail. They can also afford to let governments take the credit if they succeed.

This is–ought argument was very frustrating for those in the 1970s and 1980s who had taken an a-disciplinary approach and had studied trends in thinking. A shift in thought was emerging, and this contained the origins of an 'is' not previously discerned; this revealed as normative, simplistic and unreal the traditional power and structural explanations of international society that had claimed the label of 'realism'. Even as late as March 1981, the *International Studies Quarterly*, the official publication of the International Studies Association, was devoted to 'world system debates'. As was stated in the conclusions to that volume: 'Virtually all of the contributors to this volume interpret world affairs structurally.' There was no significant mention of behavioural aspects of relationships—despite ethnic and minority wars, terrorism, assassinations and violence across State boundaries that had little to do with structures. It was ten years out of date in terms of trends in the inter-disciplinary literature even before it was published! This was the nature of political science: insufficient resources were devoted to it and prejudices and cultural orientations were influential. A sound behavioural theory and an appropriate methodology could have been the remedy; but this remedy was not even possible when political scientists in the United States and the Soviet Union were perceiving the world from their thermonuclear power politics point of view. They did not seem to have the ability to stand back from the power conflicts in which their governments were involved and to place them in the wider context of behavioural relations. As Lester Pearson of Canada observed at the United Nations Charter Conference in 1945, the Great Powers may have had a monopoly of violence; but it did not follow that they had a monopoly of wisdom!

Some Propositions and Conclusions

In this letter it has been argued that the time-honoured problem of public policies can now be solved: at long last political and social scientists—and practitioners—can escape from the dilemma, on the one hand, of endeavouring to be 'objective' and scientific and, on the other, of resting finally on a value or a belief system.

Until the 1980s the goals of human endeavour and of societies rested on contending claims of consensus, claims made by class, religious, ideological and other pressure groups. The common components of a consensus—components such as 'justice', 'equality' and 'freedom'—were accordingly defined in ways that reflected interests and viewpoints. Means of achieving these ends—'democracy', 'socialism' and 'communism'—were none the less given a meaning and a justification that accorded with the value system and philosophy of the user. As a consequence, contending ideologies and religions, championed by men and women of indubitable idealism and conviction, have, from time to time in the history of civilization, led to massive violence, repression and exploitation and, continually, in all societies and at all social and political levels, to adversary institutions and confrontations.

In the closing decades of the twentieth century, political and social scientists—practitioners—had knowledge of the existence of human needs, needs that are universal and pursued universally and which, for this reason, provide objective guides as to goals and fixed navigation points by which they may reliably be pursued. There is now a means of objectively assessing the validity of policies in relation to human goals and of assessing, too, the efficacy of means by which they may be pursued.

We were groping toward this intellectual millennium for a long time. Indeed, the personal value systems that were reflected in ideologies and in religions always implied an acknowledgement of the 'genuinely human' (Zetterbaum, 1977) that has to be taken into account in the management of harmonious societies. Many authors pointed to specific goals and aspirations that were, in their view, fundamental and universal. *Why Men Rebel, When Men Revolt and Why*—all men, at all times, in all societies—were typical titles that acknowledged this generality (Gurr, 1970; Davis, 1971).

However, there was a marked tendency for scholars to be reductionist and to focus on those aspects of the total problem that happened to appeal to them. Marx seemed to anticipate a progressive degeneration in economic conditions that would finally provoke men and women to revolt, implying that there is some kind of human response to deprivation. De Tocqueville seemed to think that improved conditions triggered aspirations and revolt. Davies focused on development followed by reversal in fortunes. Gurr was interested in relative deprivation. Groups of scholars functioning within particular disciplines no less had their own special definitions of political and social problems, to the exclusion of many other aspects. Psychologists had their own theories (for example, aggression theories); sociologists focused on power, class and stratification; lawyers on means of control; students of politics on decision-making processes and political structures. A synthesis was elusive. There were increased knowledge and insights; but there did not emerge any general theories or guides to public policy or means of assessing policies.

In the 1970s, however, the general and undefined became more specific, thanks to work in two largely separate research areas. First and foremost there was the area of growth and learning which revealed a set of needs relating, not to the individual as an entity that required air, water and food, but to the individual as a unit part of a social system that required and would acquire, regardless of cost to self and system, specific opportunities for development (Box, 1971). The significance for political and social scientists—and for practitioners —is that unless these conditions are met, societies cannot be harmonious. The second research area was that of sociobiology, which revealed what, in retrospect, was to be expected: human societies and the behaviour of units within them, have antecedents no less than the physical human organism. Whether the patterns revealed by sociobiology are literally and solely genetic or not, is not of immediate interest to the political and social scientists—or to practitioners. It is the existence of patterned behaviour that is politically and socially significant.

Both of these research areas were influenced by empirical observation—the political realities of ethnicity and identity and struggles for independence and participation. Both were also influenced by Western thought and culture, which was characterized by the conflict between institutional and human values. It is this non-reductionist, philosophical and interdisciplinary approach that turned out to be compelling. Bay (1958) sought in his widely interpreted 'freedom goal' a 'useful guide to policies'. What he then said with caution was spelt out by the 1970s in sufficient detail to justify the removal of policy from an ideological battle-ground (Burton, 1979).

By way of summary, I list below some relevant propositions.

Human needs

(i) There are human needs that range from the basic requirements of life to social experience such as security, recognition, control and stimulus.

(ii) These needs relate to learning and development: they are needs, the satisfaction of which is a pre-condition to the growth of the individual as a unit member of a society.

(iii) Such human needs have a genetic base and are also acquired in the sense that they are generated by the experience of living within a society.

(iv) It can be deduced that the needs are universal; but that the behaviour to which they lead takes on varieties of forms according to different experience in different societies.

(v) Such human needs, being fundamental to the requirements of growth and of the individual as a social being, are pursued inexorably despite legal and social constraints and in the long term find political and social expression.

(vi) It follows that in conditions in which needs are unattainable the individual will find expression taking the forms of anti-social or abnormal behaviour.

Political relevance

(vii) These needs were not studied or given consideration in public policy because they did not call for study or concern in conditions in which an authority was in a power position to regulate behaviour, according to legal and social norms, in the interests, as perceived by it, of society as a whole.
(viii) Such human needs will be politically and socially significant in the future because of technological and environmental changes generally that have altered the relative political power of authorities and those governed, giving greater opportunity for the pursuit of human needs by dissent, protest and violence.
(ix) Policies that run counter to the pursuit of such human needs will, therefore, be counter-productive.
(x) It can be deduced that such human needs, being universal, are a requirement of elites no less than others and that, therefore, role defence is to be anticipated no less than role acquisition in conditions of political change.
(xi) Counter-productivity is in the short term, therefore, not a discouragement to elites, even though it makes inevitable the application by them of coercion and violent opposition.
(xii) In the long term counter-productivity and its costs to elite values forces reconsideration of policies and the pursuit of those that are less subjective ideologically, and interest inspired.

Human needs as guide to policy

(xiii) Means of pursuing political goals, in addition to the goals themselves, can also be assessed and guided by reference to human needs.
(xiv) Reactive decision-making processes whether judicial,

mediatory, or bargaining, themselves impose constraints and prejudice outcomes, frequently excluding consideration of human needs.

(xv) Reactive decision-making processes make puzzles out of problems by ignoring or reducing by coercion behavioural variables that can be suppressed only temporarily.

(xvi) Effective decision-making processes are not the reactive, closed system, trial and error, cybernetic, strategic ones depicted and encouraged by social scientists, but are inter-active and problem solving in the sense that behavioural needs and responses in open systems are taken into account.

Conflict resolution

(xvii) Human societal needs, being non-material, are increased by consumption (the more identity and security someone experiences, the more others experience, making positive-sum, non-distributive, outcomes possible).

(xviii) The fact that universal human needs include non-material goals that are in infinite supply, opens up means of resolving apparent zero-sum conflicts of interest, including problems of change by positive-sum outcomes and, therefore, without violence or coercion.

(xix) The State and sovereignty, legal authority, legitimate monopoly of force, are not useful tools of analysis. The nation and small group, legitimization, values attached to relationships are tools more relevant to problem-solving within and between national groups.

(xx) Problem-solving processes and techniques are available that involve parties to disputes along with third parties employing such tools, that lead to agreed definitions of relationship and to agreed outcomes.

Conclusion

Such guide lines to policy having been set down, it has to be stressed that the only political models which civilizations

THE LETTER

have had are power models. These will dominate until consensual understanding alters, until inter-active decision making institutions are established. This being the case the guide lines apply to a Second Track that will compete for status, influence and effectiveness in the conduct of human affairs, one that can be supported and promoted by authorities which are pursuing the first track, one that finally makes irrelevant the power track—for it is only by making power irrelevant that it can be controlled.

The Second Track comprises inter-active information gathering, inter-active decision making, inter-active research on both domestic and international problems and inter-active problem solving and conflict resolving institutions. If it is impossible for authorities to initiate and to promote a Second Track for fear that this could signal weakness, then informal means of inter-action can be undertaken through third parties.

In short, as you emerge you will be faced with the immediate tasks of cleaning up and of reconstruction. You will tend to reconstruct on the basis of the past, past institutions, past values, past relationships. This is inevitable, no matter how much you plan to do otherwise: the immediate cleaning up tasks will lead into longer term policies and approaches. The first track will dominate once again. Institutional logical imperatives will control you. Consequently, you have no option, if another catastrophe is to be avoided, but to pursue the Second Track and signal most clearly to all concerned that wherever you might be pressed to go on the first track, you are at the same time prepared to put a lot of energy and resources into progress along the Second Track.

There are many other matters I should have liked to raise. The pre-holocaust period was, as you know, a pleasant one for a small elite in poor societies and for a large middle class in the wealthy societies. However, it was an inhuman, almost animal-like existence for the great bulk of the human race.

DEAR SURVIVORS

We closed our minds to this—almost forgotten were the near-starving refugees by the million deprived of relationships and living a life of squalor and physical deprivation, peoples living under oppressive authorities that placed their status and role before the human needs of their peoples. These underlying conditions were an essential cause of what eventually led to catastrophe, though we did not wish to acknowledge this—recognition of these tensions would have forced us to consider radical, national and international changes in authority structures and distributions of wealth and opportunities.

However, I did not touch on these things in this letter because they were a symptom of failure. Conflict avoidance and the solution of these problems is deeper. Political reality in a nuclear age is not the relative power of States and people, but the obligation to satisfy human needs by solving human problems without resort to a coercive political system. Even when you take the first steps at cleaning up and organizing survivors, remember that the elite society is self-destroying. We know that now. Participation, recognition, identity, development for all, are not the constituent parts of an ideology. They are the politically realistic constituents of any on-going society.

With good wishes and concern.

John Burton

BIBLIOGRAPHY

Ardrey, R. (1966), *The Territorial Imperative*, London, Collins/Fontana.
Barash, D. P. (1977), *Sociology and Behaviour*, Oxford, Elsevier.
Bay, C. (1958), *The Structure of Freedom*, Stanford University Press.
Bernstein, R. J. (1976), *The Restructuring of Social and Political Theory*, Oxford, Blackwell.
Blau, P. (1964), *Exchange and Power in Social Life*, New York, Wiley.
Bodenheimer, E. (1971), 'Philosophical anthropology and the law', *California Law Review*, Vol. 59, No. 3.
Boulding, K. (1970), *A Primer of Social Dynamics*, New York, Free Press.
Boulding, K. (1978), *Ecodynamics*, London, Sage.
Brecht, A. (1959), *Political Theory*, Cambridge, Mass., Princeton University Press.
Burns, J. M. (1977), 'Wellsprings of political leadership', *American Political Science Review, 1977*.
Burton, J. W. (1969), *Conflict or Communication*, Basingstoke, Macmillan.
Burton, J. W. (1979), *Deviance, Terrorism and War*, Oxford, Martin Robertson.
David Davis Memorial Institute (1963), *Report on Peaceful Settlement of International Disputes*.
Davis, J. C. (ed.) (1971), *When Men Revolt and Why*, New York, Free Press.
Davis, J. C. (1979), 'Communication', *American Political Science Review*, Vol. 73, No. 3.
D'Entreves, A. (1970), *Natural Law*, London, Hutchinson.
Deutsch, K. (1963), *The Nerves of Government*, New York, Free Press.
Easton, D. (1965), *A Systems Analysis of Political Life*, New York, Wiley.
Easton, D. (1969), 'The new revolution in political science', *The American Political Science Review, 1969*.
Enloe, C. (1973), *Ethnic Conflict and Political Developments*, Boston, Little, Brown & Co.

Epstein, A. L. (1978), *Ethos and Identity*, London, Tavistock.
Glazer, N. and Moyneham, D. P. (eds) (1975), *Ethnicity*, Harvard University Press.
Gurr, T. R. (ed.) (1977), *The Politics of Crime and Conflict*, London, Sage.
Gurr, T. R. (1979), *Why Men Rebel*, Cambridge, Mass., Princeton University Press.
Himmelweil, S. (1977), 'The individual as basic limb of analysis', in Green, F. and Nore, P. (eds), *Economics: An Anti-Text*, Basingstoke, Macmillan.
Johnson, C. (1966), *Revolutionary Change*, Boston, Little, Brown & Co.
Kelman, H. C. (1972), 'The problem-solving workshop in conflict resolution', in Merritt, R. L. (ed.), *Communication in International Relations*.
Kelman, H. C. and Cohen, S. (1976), 'The problem-solving workshop', *Journal of Peace Research*, Vol. XIII, No. 2.
Knutson, I. N. (ed.) (1973), *Handbook of Political Psychology*, London, Jossey-Bass.
Kuhn, T. S. (1962), *The Structure of Scientific Revolutions*, Chicago, Chicago University Press.
Landau, M. (1972), *Political Theory and Political Science*, Brighton, Harvester Press.
Le Vine, R. A. and Campbell, D. T. (1972), *Ethnocentrism: Theories of Conflict, Ethnic Attitudes and Group Behaviour*, New York, Wiley.
Levi, I. (1980), 'Introduction to science', in Mellor, D. H. (ed.), *Science, Relief & Behaviour*, Cambridge, Cambridge University Press.
Lloyd, D. (1964), *The Idea of Law*, Harmondsworth, Penguin Books.
Maslow, A. H. (1954), *Motivation and Personality*, New York, Harper Bros.
Mitchell, C. R. (1981), *Peacemaking and the Consultant's Role*, London, Gower Press.
Modelski, G. (1962), *A Theory of Foreign Policy*, London, Pall Mall Press.
Pepinsky, H. E. (1976), *Crime and Conflict*, Oxford, Martin Robertson.
Peretz, P. (1978), 'Universal wants: a deductive framework for comparative political analysis', in Ashford, D. E. (ed.), *Comparing Public Policies: New Concepts and Methods*, London, Sage.
Popper, K. (1957), *The Poverty of Historicism*, London, Routledge & Kegan Paul.
Rokeach, M. (1974), *Beliefs, Attitudes and Values*, San Francisco, Jossey-Bass.

BIBLIOGRAPHY

Scarman, L. (1977), 'Human rights', University of London Bulletin, No. 39.

Scruton, R. (1980), *The Meaning of Conservatism*, Harmondsworth, Penguin Books.

Sites, P. (1973), *Control, the Basis of Social Order*, New York, Dunellen Publishers.

Stern, D. (1977), *The First Relationship: Infant and Mother*, London, Collins/Fontana.

Truman, D. (1978), 'The impact of political science on the revolution in the behavioural sciences', in Brodbeck, M. (ed.), *Readings in the Philosophies of Social Sciences*, New York, Appleton–Century–Crofts.

USA Peace Academy (1978), Public Law 95-561, November 19 1978.

Wedge, B. (1971), 'A psychiatric model for intercession in inter-group conflict', *The Journal of Applied Behavioural Science*, Vol. 6, No. 7.

Weiner, B. (1979), *Human Motivation*, London, Holt Rinehart & Winston.

Wilson, E. O. (1975), *Sociology*, Harvard University Press.

Winch, P. (1958), *The Idea of Social Sciences and its Relation to Philosophy*, London, Routledge & Kegan Paul.

Zetterbaum, M. (1977), 'Equality and human need', *American Political Science Review*, Vol. LXXI, No. 3.